THE
DREAMWORK
HANDBOOK

THE
DREAMWORK
HANDBOOK

Transform your
life through dreams

WATKINS
Sharing Wisdom Since 1893

DR NICHOLAS HEYNEMAN

The Dreamwork Handbook
Nicholas Heyneman

First published in the UK in 2000 as *Dreams & Relationships* by Duncan Baird Publishers Ltd.

This edition published in the UK and USA in 2022 by Watkins, an imprint of Watkins Media Limited, Unit 11, Shepperton House, 83–93 Shepperton Road London N1 3DF

enquiries@watkinspublishing.com

Commissioning Editor: Ella Chappell
Assistant Editor: Brittany Willis
Head of Design: Karen Smith
Designer: Kieryn Tyler
Cover Design: Fra Corsini
Production: Uzma Taj

A CIP record for this book is available from the British Library

ISBN: 978-1-84899-258-0 (Hardback)
ISBN: 978-1-84899-259-7 (eBook)

10 9 8 7 6 5 4 3 2 1

Printed in United Kingdom by TJ Books Ltd

www.watkinspublishing.com

Publisher's note: The information presented in this book about dreams is educational in nature and is provided only as general information and is not medical or psychological advice nor is it intended as a substitute for licensed health care services. The author and publisher shall have neither responsibility nor liability to any person or entity with respect to any loss, damage, or injury caused or alleged to be caused directly or indirectly by the information contained in this book, including journal practices and exercises.

CONTENTS

INTRODUCTION

Sometime over the next several hours, you will go to bed, fall asleep and travel to a universe where time and logic no longer exist, where there are no limits to what you may experience, and where random and bizarre images dance before your eyes. You will do this tonight and every night, spending over six years of your life in this state of consciousness. I am speaking, of course, of dreams.

What are these mysterious night-time dramas? Why do we experience them? Does everyone dream? And, perhaps the most important question of all — do dreams offer insight, help solve problems and enrich our relationships? These questions are not new, but dreamwork has evolved over the years and this book brings a contemporary and very personal perspective to understanding the baffling images that entertain us each night.

Dreamwork is the thoughtful development of hypotheses about ourselves by deciphering the language of dreams. It allows us to glimpse our true feelings unconstrained by the mental censor that is continually active while we are awake, such as now, as you read these words. Dreamwork offers a potent tool for self-understanding, empowering us to make better decisions about ourselves, improve our relationships and strengthen our resolve to conquer the challenges presented by life.

The Dreamwork Handbook is a new and completely revised edition of *How Dreams Can Enrich Your Relationships*. We will discuss how dreams are a continuation of waking thoughts and feelings, with meaning that can only be understood through the unique lens of each person's life, and also how some dreams connect our consciousness with the consciousness of others. We will make clear connections between the seemingly nonsensical images of our nightly dreams and events in daily life, and discuss why a particular dream makes its appearance at the time that it does.

This book is intended to be a hands-on experience that will take you through the entire process of dream interpretation, from remembering your dreams and discovering their meaning to applying these results to your daily life. There are sections on:

- ★ understanding what emotions mean in dreams

- ★ how dreams can impact relationships

- ★ exploring the spiritual aspects of dreaming

- ★ how to change your dreams to make them more beneficial

- ★ how to co-dream with others

WHAT CAN YOU EXPECT?

The Dreamwork Handbook includes numerous examples and thought-provoking exercises to help guide your journey.

Chapter one presents an overview of dreaming and the various approaches to exploring dreamwork. We will discuss why dreams seem strange and how to translate the unique language of dreams. We will also explain the role of emotions in dreaming, with new ways to look at dream symbols.

Chapter two contains everything you need to learn to remember your dreams. It includes detailed dream recall strategies and exercises that will take you from not remembering a single dream to recalling your dreams almost every night. This chapter will teach you how to keep a meaningful dream journal by learning to recognize what is (and is not) important to record. There are plenty of places in this book set aside for you to journal your dreams, jot down notes or doodle dream images.

Chapter three dives into the heart of dream interpretation. This chapter is more workbook than textbook offering hands-on experience in peeling away the layers of dreaming's mysterious images to reveal the insight-laden symbols of nearly every dream you experience.

Chapter four's content is more advanced, but by this point you will be ready for it. Using examples and exercises, you will learn you how to seed your dreams to help solve specific problems, how to lucid dream and how to co-dream with a partner or friend.

Chapter five explores some of the most common emotions found in dreams, why they come up and practical ways to apply what you learn to your daily life.

Chapter six is an in-depth look at using dreams to enrich your relationships. This section is relevant for all kinds of relationships – lovers, family, friends and coworkers. We will harness dreaming in original ways to help communicate with a friend or partner and to face relationship challenges. We will peek into the meaning of erotic dreams and explore playful yet powerful ways to build intimacy.

Chapter seven presents a method to actively explore the process of dream interpretation using daydreams. Guided daydreaming can help you to think differently about your dreams and walk you through the process of dream interpretation.

Chapter eight is a brief symbol guide. This chapter lists some of the most common symbols found in dreams to provide a starting point for understanding them. Dreams are highly personal so no dream dictionary can tell what your dream means, but the prompts in this chapter can offer a useful place to begin thinking about more puzzling dreams.

The Dreamwork Handbook is intended to be an engaging and thought-provoking experience, but of course it is not a source of professional therapy. Dreamwork is a fun, enlightening and very personal journey. No one can interpret your dreams for you, but you can learn to navigate the strange universe that you visit each night. My hope is that you will find, as I do, that dreamwork is a transformative process that adds a depth and richness to your life.

CHAPTER

1

WHAT ARE DREAMS?

Through the ages, philosophers and scientists alike have debated the nature of dreaming and as in every debate there are extreme positions. Some scientists assert that dreaming is nothing more than random electrical activity produced by the brain when we sleep, or that dreaming functions only to flush out surplus stimulation that has accumulated over the course of a day, or to strip emotion from memories. Yet many philosophers and shaman believe that dreams can be a source of profound truths, prophecies and even supernatural powers. Or they are a demonstration that the soul leaves the body to experience life elsewhere.

Not surprisingly, most psychologists fall somewhere between these two poles, proposing that dreams can't extend our natural human faculties, but they can illuminate our innermost self. How do we harness this insight?

We now know that dreams are less random and more organized than originally thought, but they do not conform to the rules of waking logic. A person may sprout wings and fly, inanimate objects walk and talk, friends, family and lovers appear and disappear in bodies we know are not their own, and none of this seems to bother us in a dream. This "dream logic" is as much at home in our sleep as rationality is in our waking minds.

We may process mental images differently when we dream, but in actuality dream logic is not as obtuse as it may appear. Take the widely experienced dream phenomena of seeing someone you know appear in a dream as a visually incongruent figure. You recognize them immediately even though they inhabit a different body. The visual depiction does not define the person – their identity does. This can easily be transferred across objects, akin to changing our appearance in waking life by wearing new clothes or getting a different hairstyle.

As an analogy, imagine someone you know and notice the first image that comes to mind. Notice their physical characteristics. If you view them from different angles they will look different, but they are still clearly recognizable. Now imagine this person in physically impossible configurations – stretched into a circle, flattened into a line with a sharp 90 degrees at their waist or twisted into a pretzel. They appear odd and perhaps amusing, but it is still them. In waking reality our core representation of a person is their identity, not their visual appearance. The same goes for dreaming.

LANGUAGE OF DREAMS

To interpret a dream we need to speak the dream's language. What immediately pops to mind for most people are the dream's images or what we refer to as symbols. We often overlook that dreams contain another vital element — emotions — the feelings embodied within a particular dream. Dream emotions provide the context to make sense of a dream's symbols. According to an array of dream dictionaries, dreaming of a train could represent a journey, an opportunity, a penis, death, expectations and many other interpretive suggestions. All or none of these may be accurate, but recognizing how the dream felt gives us a good start in sorting through the various possibilities.

Emotions form the epicentre of a dream, creating a map to navigate our experience. Does the dream feel frightening? Serene? Erotic? When you wake are you plunged into a similar emotional state? Does it remind you of something from your past?

Generally speaking, dream emotions accurately reflect our waking emotions even if they are buried behind a wall of conscious denial. If a dream feels anxious, it is most likely telling us to look for meaning in past or present events associated with this feeling, or perhaps there is a future event that we may be facing with more disquieting anticipation than we are consciously aware of.

Waking consciousness protects us from emotional assaults by automatically triggering psychological barriers that allow only feelings we can manage. Others are censored, but may arise when we sleep. Dream emotions are straightforward, sometimes brutally honest, making them the ideal starting point for interpreting their personal meaning. If a dream is a story and symbols are the words, then the emotions of a dream are the grammar that give the story meaning.

Dreams tend to be polarized, either pleasant or distressful, and invariably some dreams will elicit uncomfortable feelings. Naturally, this book is not intended as a source of therapy. Always seek out a therapist if you find an experience distressing or worrisome.

Exercise: How to create an emotional dream map

In many instances, it is helpful to create an emotional dream map to organize your interpretative approach. For example, say your dream was about winning the lottery. There are many ways this dream could be interpreted, but let us look at one dimension – the dream may represent themes of wealth, freedom and security or it may indicate fear, harassment and loss. To explore and organize possible dream emotions, try these steps:

1. Bring the dream narrative back into your mind. Ask yourself what the dream feels like — first the overall emotions of the dream, then any feelings associated with specific dream images.

2. Note any information that may be helpful to capture the dream's emotional experience. You could draw small pictures or doodles. We will discuss this in more detail in the next chapter when we talk about creating a dream journal.

3. Once you feel your recollection is complete, draw a visual representation in your dream.

   ★ Toward the top of the page, write down the overriding emotion of the dream.

   ★ Circle this word and draw lines radiating off it like the rays coming from the sun.

   ★ At the end of each line, write any additional emotions you experienced, sizing the words proportionally to the intensity of the feeling.

   ★ Attach a note or doodle indicating which dream character expressed which emotion.

   ★ Also note any conflicting emotions if you notice them (such as confidence versus insecurity) and the dream characters representing them.

4. Jot down any specific dream symbols that seem particularly connected to a given feeling and draw a line to attach the feeling to the symbol.

5. Next, below the diagram you have just drawn, fill in what you are feeling now, in bed in the morning, while you are mapping your dream. Make some quick notes.

★ How are these waking feelings similar or different from those in your dream?

★ When you are recalling the dream, does it make you feel happy, sad, anxious, and so on?

★ Do the emotions feel bodily, like anxiousness in the pit of your stomach or a feeling of emptiness in your solar plexus region?

★ Do any of these feelings seem associated with something in your daily waking life or from your past?

An emotional map serves two purposes. You can use it as a tool to catalogue the emotional contents of your dream life and also to clarify the nuances of a feeling. If you intuitively sense there are feelings you may have missed, that you can't quite put your finger on, try bringing the dream back into your mind and follow any dream characters that seem to be most associated with this missing emotion.

Bear in mind that words often fail to capture the emotional spectrum of experience. Anyone who has been in love will tell you the word love is a woefully inadequate description of the experience. Probing dream feelings adds emotional breadth and meaning to an interpretation.

Once we have become practised at recognizing a dream's emotional content, we can then begin to decipher the symbolic language of a dream. Dream images are the easily recognizable pictures in your dreams – a human, monkey, clown, hooded knight, and so on, even if these are oddly configured (for example, the head of a human attached to the body of an animal).

Finally, visual images do not behave the same in dreams as they would do in waking life; it is the dream emotions that tie meaning together. Dreams are nothing like a film. There is no beginning, middle or end. It is impossible to walk into the middle of a dream. There is no space, no time and no logic that we take for granted while awake. Longer dreams can be split up into fragments and interpreted. In fact, this is almost always what we are doing in dreamwork – focusing on parts of a dream.

DREAM SYMBOLISM

While emotions form the nucleus of a dream, symbols add substance. The pioneer of psychoanalysis, Sigmund Freud, likened human consciousness to an iceberg floating in the ocean: the relatively small projection above the waterline represents waking reality (consciousness), while the massive body of the iceberg lying below the surface is our mysterious and complex unconscious.

Before we begin to use dreams to enhance our relationships, we need to understand what may lie beneath the surface of the ocean of consciousness, and how that understanding can help. Freud's student-turned-rival, Carl Jung, divided this vast expanse of the unconscious into two components: the personal unconscious and the collective unconscious.

Jung believed that the collective unconscious houses the emotional, intellectual and spiritual experiences of every human being who has lived before us. It is the part of our mind that we all have in common, made up of the instincts, fears, appetites, myths and symbols woven into the very fabric of the common ancestral mind. He believed that the collective unconscious extends the reach of our awareness and connects us to one another at the deepest level.

ARCHETYPES

Jung gave the term "archetypes" to symbols with universally laden meaning that reside in the collective unconscious. These are not fully formed images themselves, but are more like the prototype on which an image can develop in a variety of ways depending on the individual. Archetypal energy underlies knowledge shared by all humans across history, and it unconsciously directs each person's behaviour. In essence, the collective unconscious is a form of shared consciousness across all people of all time. Such themes appear ubiquitously in literature, drama, art, religion – and of course in dreams.

Not all dreams contain archetypes, and the ones that do are often described as having a spiritual, numinous quality that feels ego dystonic, meaning not originating from us – the dreamer – but possessed of a deeper, wiser, spiritual feel. Archetypal dreams inspire personal growth. Some people believe that these are the basis for all human advancement – a foundation of previous knowledge.

It is often helpful to pay attention to archetypal dreams as they may provide opportunities to expand our consciousness and personal growth and deepen our connections to others. Jung believed there are as many archetypes as life situations, but a few seem to emerge most frequently.

The persona

The personal archetype is a mask or façade that we wear, enabling us to share with the world only what we wish others to see. It is our public presentation, which may not be anything like who we truly are. Naturally, we expose ourselves only in a socially acceptable manner. The persona is quite different from being fake; it is an integral part of being human and necessary for survival. It would be chaos if we all publicly displayed every unconscious detail of ourselves. However, overidentifying with the persona may result in our losing sight of our true self.

The persona archetype may be symbolized by just about any dream image. Look first for the overall tone of the dream as an indication of its archetypal symbolism, then look for specific symbols that feel like they portray the dream character in a particular fashion, perhaps unidimensional. We typically possess multiple masks so there may be several persona symbols within a dream.

The hero

This archetype overcomes obstacles so that we are able to achieve a specific goal. He is our warrior that clears the way for us to advance. The hero often faces physical challenges or ones that require skill and courage. In dreams, the hero is an action-oriented character – fighting, climbing and problem-solving. The hero finds the treasure we are searching for, saves the damsel in distress, and discovers the elixir of life. The hero is a metaphor for our psychological journey on a quest to develop our unique potential.

The shadow

The shadow embodies our primitive nature and the dark, repressed and aggressive parts of ourselves that we wish to keep hidden away. Much of the shadow archetype derives from repressed material, often too frightening for even our conscious self to become aware of. The nefarious aspects of our personality, our basic instincts, are always within us, buried deep in the unconscious. But just because they are out of mind does not mean they no longer exist. The shadow is persistent and can never be vanquished; the repressed contents of the unconscious are as much a part of us as the attention you are using now to read these words. Nor would we want to banish the shadow. It is a vital source of energy, creativity and ingenuity that allows us to overcome all kinds of barriers. Herein lies the dilemma: stifle the shadow too much and we lose the energy and creativity necessary to face a challenge in the first place; allow the shadow a free hand and it will surely conflict with our innate sense of right and wrong.

To lessen our inner conflict and feel more at peace with ourselves, we need to understand the shadow element of our psyche, and this is where dreamwork is of great value. Through an understanding of dreams, we can view our dark side, beneficially assimilate it into our overall self, and become aware of when we are behaving in a manner overly associated with this archetype.

The trickster

The trickster is a sly dream character who likes to play annoying games that sometimes wreak havoc. This archetype may not seem to have value, at least in the moment, but actually benefits us by symbolizing a switch from conventional to more intuitive approaches to problem-solving. As such, dream characters that transform themselves within a dream may represent the trickster.

The mother

This archetype symbolizes our nurturing, caring self that nourishes growth. The mother archetype also has an opposite side: possessiveness, and jealousy, and is ruthlessly protective.

In dreams, the mother can be a powerful force regardless of the gender of the dreamer.

Although Jung proposed several archetypes, some dream workers propose that the list be extended to include other images that evoke associations in all of us. For example, fire and snake seem to have universal connotations: fire is passion, warmth and survival but with the potential for destruction or hurt (the connections with relationships are obvious); the snake may suggest venom or loss of innocence (the biblical tempter).

PERSONAL UNCONSCIOUS

The personal unconscious is the reservoir of emotions, knowledge, attitudes and beliefs that we accumulate through personal experience. Although genetic factors may play a part, the personal unconscious is largely formed by a lifetime of interactions – the essence of each and every past experience is distilled and assimilated into the unconscious mind, gelling and shaping what we call our personality.

Ultimately, most dream symbols are personal – an image that holds a unique and personalized message derived from our individual unconscious minds. Many people dream of birds, but no two dream-birds share the same interpretive meaning. Dream symbols often comprise several layers of meaning ranging from literal to highly associative. Consider the symbol of a gold coin.

Literal

In waking reality, gold coins are an indication of wealth. But in dreams such a literal interpretation is rare. Dreaming of a pot of gold coins does not mean you are rich or are going to be rich.

Symbolic

Gold coins represent a less tangible value. Perhaps they could indicate a quest of some kind: a search for happiness, a relationship or independence.

Associative

This is the most common interpretation for a gold coin. It may seem confusing, but bear with me – it can mean anything! Put another way, the meaning of a coin, like any symbol, is based upon the dreamer's personal experience. Many factors may play a role – the coin's physical properties, social conventions (like a wedding ring), mythological roots – but all of these depend on whichever association the dreamer makes.

Take the following dream fragment: "I dreamt I found a gold coin on the railroad track and suddenly felt scared and alone." Why would finding a gold coin make the dreamer feel scared and lonely?

When the dreamer explored his dream, he remembered that as a child he found a coin on a railroad track that looked gold but was not gold. The dream was associated with a troubling time in his life and he experienced similar feelings to those he experienced during those times. Then he remembered a vaguely similar feeling cropping up recently, not intense enough to disturb him or remind him of the past, but enough to complicate work challenges he was facing. The dream coin, then, is neither gold nor valuable, but is a reminder of long-past negative emotions. The lesson here is that a symbol is only meaningful to the dreamer; no one else can interpret it.

CONTEMPORARY APPROACHES TO DREAMWORK

Contemporary dreamwork draws less on unique symbol types, but instead views dreams as a continuation of waking thoughts and feelings. Dreams may represent our aspirations and concerns, something related to our past, or they may reflect events that occurred only hours before we fall asleep.

Dream images are considered to be mental representations of objects and actions in the waking world. Even if the image is convoluted, as it often is in a dream, it still represents something that is describable. For example, the dream image of a man with the head of a turtle does not exist in waking life, but men and turtles do. A creeping dream blob may not represent anything real in life, but it is still recognizable enough for us to call it a blob.

Dream symbols refer to the meaning we attach to dream images. Images are what you see and are fixed; the symbolic meaning that we attach can vary greatly. For example, the image of an ocean is always an ocean (even if it is floating in space), but it may symbolize life, beginnings, renewal, birth or many other things depending upon the dreamer. For simplicity, the two terms are sometimes used synonymously.

Dreams have uniquely personal meanings and can only be understood through the lens of the dreamer's past history, present life and even their daily experiences. This means that dreaming of a horse last night may have one interpretation, but dreaming of it again tonight may represent something entirely different. So how do we make sense of a dream image if its meaning can change from night to night? The answer is surprisingly straightforward and brings us back to where we began in this chapter: placing the dream's image into its emotional context to help us understand the symbolism.

Recent events may trigger an emotional response: for example, an argument with our partner or witnessing an automobile accident. But dream feelings can also originate from the more distant past, particularly childhood. If the emotions we experience are powerful enough, they may never vanish, and some leave an indelible mark. This means we need to learn to distinguish emotions that originate in our present lives and those from our past. The gold coin on the railway track mentioned above is a good example of a dream triggered by past feelings. Dream emotions will be explored in depth throughout this book.

In addition to dream emotions, some contemporary approaches to dreamwork are concerned with the automatic thoughts generated in response to recalling a dream. Automatic thoughts are self-statements that spontaneously pop into our head. They are usually short, flash through the mind quickly, are self-referent and can be self-critical. They are sometimes difficult to spot because they are so transient, but they can have a big impact on how we feel about ourselves. For example, if we make a mistake, a barely registered thought may say something like, "I can't do anything right." It is often gone before we notice it was there, but it leaves us feeling bad about ourselves, despite being inaccurate (there is no such person who can't do anything right).

In dreamwork, we can learn to recognize self-statements that come up when we are remembering a dream and use these to help us understand ourselves better. Our self-statements may help us to gain insight into self-esteem, unwanted habits or how we interact with others. We can then apply this knowledge to modify our thinking which, in turn, may lead to behaviour change. Some may argue that we are using conscious strategies to modify unconscious patterns.

At first, dreaming may seem incompatible with waking logic, but ultimately our various states of consciousness synergize each other – the unconscious breadth of dreaming complements our waking rationality and commonsense.

In the pages that follow, we are going to use dreamwork to develop thoughtful hypotheses about ourselves, find creative ways to improve decision-making, enhance our relationships and strengthen our resolve to conquer the challenges presented by life.

NOTES

_____

_____

_____

_____

_____

_____

_____

_____

_____

_____

_____

_____

_____

_____

CHAPTER

2

HOW TO REMEMBER YOUR DREAMS

Dreams are often elusive — the compelling dramas that filled our conscious at night will quickly fade as we shift from sleep to waking consciousness. We likely only remember a small fraction of what we dream, and while we do not know why this is, there are different possible explanations.

Some psychoanalysts believe that we immediately repress our dreams when we wake from sleep because the material they represent is too traumatic for our conscious awareness. Eventually this repressed material usually seeps into consciousness, but over time and in measured amounts. Most contemporary neuroscientists have proposed alternate models of why we forget dreams so easily. For example, we may experience a sort of amnesia resulting from lowered amounts of neurotransmitters required to convert short-term memories into longer ones.

Another explanation is simply that humans are very good at forgetting things that we deem nonessential, not just in dreams but in waking life as well. In cultures where dreaming is highly valued, dream recall is nearly universal. Traditionally, the Asabano people of Papua New Guinea endowed dreams with vital significance including evidence that supports their beliefs about everything from death and the afterlife to the conditions necessary for a successful hunt. Some Native American beliefs hold that dreams access a higher form of consciousness that guide our lives.

If we are not invested in dreams or consider them to be only fanciful stories, then we are not likely to remember them. A critical first step in remembering a dream is to adopt an attitude that dreamwork is worthy of your time and effort. Behaviour sways belief, so acting as if dreaming is helpful will enhance your success. You are doing this now by reading this book. The importance of being receptive to dreams can't be overstated if you were raised in a culture that does not prize dreaming. Remember you are fighting a deeply ingrained cultural bias that impacts us even if we are not consciously aware of it.

Another simple but important reason why you might not remember your dreams is that you have never tried to do this. That is, really tried. Remembering dreams is a skill and like any skill it takes time and effort to master. A casual attempt here and there may not be sufficient.

Stress is a factor in just about everyone's life. Being too rushed, worried, frustrated or busy in waking life makes it difficult to sleep, influences the natural quality of dreaming and can make dream recall more difficult.

GETTING A GOOD NIGHT'S SLEEP

Good quality sleep promotes physical and mental wellbeing and is a critical first step for remembering dreams. The better you sleep, the more natural meaning will appear in dreams and the more likely you will be to remember them.

Many factors can affect sleep and dreams. Various pre-sleep factors, particularly evening stimulation, can impact dreaming. What we read, watch on television or the video games we play may all impact dream recall and images. If you are susceptible it may not be a good idea to watch a horror movie right before bed.

During our sleep, sounds, smells, room temperature and flashing lights can influence dreams. We often weave these stimuli into a dream – if you are freezing in a dream your sleeping environment may be too cold, just not enough to wake you. As simple as it sounds, your sleep conditions should be noted in your dream journal.

Sleep disorders and other medical conditions, medicines, psychological states such as anxiety or depression, or being ill can all impact dreams. Some people describe medicine- or illness-related dreams as thick, boggy, blurry, slower than usual or just feeling different from what is typical for them.

Sleep preparation and sleep environment are both important factors for most people to sleep well. This is called "sleep hygiene" — behavioural patterns that promote healthy, productive sleep.

SLEEP HYGIENE

There are several main ways to establish good sleep hygiene.

1. Maintaining a regular schedule is one of the most important aspects of good sleep hygiene. A consistent pattern of bedtime and wake times helps to regulate circadian rhythms (the internal body clock). Try to keep these times as consistent as possible, even on weekends. Some people are so proficient at sleep hygiene that they no longer need an alarm clock.

2. Get at least seven hours of sleep per night. This varies by age and individual, but on average fewer than seven hours seems to be associated with increased health problems and behavioural inefficiency.

3. Exercise is beneficial for sleep and, for many people, should be done earlier in the day rather than later. As a rule of thumb, try to finish exercising three to four hours before bedtime so that you are not too energized to fall asleep.

4. Some people can nap without disturbing night-time sleep. While naps are not inherently problematic, sleep experts generally suggest avoiding them as napping may make it more difficult for you to fall asleep at night. Sleep is a homeostatic drive – the longer you are awake, the sleepier you get. A good analogy offered by one sleep scientist was to think of sleepiness as a balloon that fills up over the course of the day, creating a pressured urge to sleep. Naps deflate the balloon and lessen the perceived need to sleep, making it more difficult to doze off at night.

5. Limit caffeine intake before bedtime. Many of us drink coffee, tea or energy drinks to relieve tiredness, but these also make it more difficult to fall asleep – even if we feel tired.

6. As mentioned above, sleep environment is critical. The temperature, light and noise level in your bedroom can disrupt sleep quality. White noise is sometimes helpful to mask abrupt and disturbing sounds that interfere with sleep, as is eliminating as many distractions as possible. A TV or computer flickering in the background can interfere with successful sleep.

7. Avoid using your phone or computer or reading stimulating material before sleep. Allow yourself to wind down at bedtime.

8. It may be helpful to develop a relaxing bedtime routine, such as taking a warm bath or using relaxation suggestions, to encourage sleepiness.

9. If you struggle to fall asleep, do not lie awake in bed beyond half an hour. Get up and sit quietly in a darkened room until you feel the urge to sleep.

Making the transition from a busy day to restorative sleep is critical for remembering dreams. Instead of dropping into bed so tired that you fall asleep instantly, it is important to spend a few moments creating a calm mental state that is receptive to dreaming. We are going to use relaxation methods, affirmations and self-hypnotic techniques.

Exercise: Pre-sleep relaxation methods

There are several relaxation methods to choose from and three of them are presented below. Pick any that work for you.

1. Lie in a comfortable position and try to disengage your mind from the thoughts of the day. Focus on your breathing. Take a slow, deep breath in through your nose so that your stomach rises but your chest does not move. Breathe out through your mouth with your lips slightly pursed (as if you were whistling). This is called diaphragmatic breathing. You can start with as few as ten breaths, taking your time with each, then notice if your body feels more relaxed.

2. Slowly scan your body beginning at the crown of your head downward to the tip of your toes. As you do, imagine a calming blue light hugging each part of your body, internal and external, until the light completely envelops you. Do not rush this process; let it move slowly and naturally and touch every part in you, inside and out.

3. Conjure up a soothing mental scene, real or imagined, that allows your body to let go of tension. For example, you may mentally travel to a place that feels soothing to you. Allow the image to envelope you as you feel the tension floating off your body and dissipating like steam into the air. Do not be frustrated by intrusive thoughts as these enter your mind – which they will – just gently sweep them away.

AFFIRMATIONS

Affirmations are short, meditative statements that you repeat to yourself, either silently in your head or softly aloud, to achieve a goal. In this case we will use them to encourage your mind to remember your dreams. Later in this book we will use affirmations to seed dreams for specific purposes, such as asking for guidance from your dreams or help in resolving a conflict.

To teach yourself to recall dreams, it is best to use affirmations following a relaxation exercise that helps to clear your mind and calm your body. Try to repeat the affirmations as close to actually falling asleep as possible as there is some evidence that the hypnagogic state (the place on the border of being awake and sleeping) is especially sensitive to suggestion.

Here are some example affirmations that can be used for dream recall, though please tailor them so they work for you:

- ★ Remembering my dreams is natural and positive.

- ★ My dreams have value for me.

- ★ I wish to become increasingly aware of my dreams.

- ★ I am open to experiencing my dreams.

- ★ I am curious about my dreams.

Whatever affirmations you choose to use, repeat them mentally or in a soft voice, like a mantra. The wording is less important than the intent; anything simple, positive and confident will work. They should make sense to you and not contradict your beliefs. For example, if the jury is still out on your belief in the value of dreaming, an affirmation that states you believe in the value of your dreams probably won't succeed.

SELF-HYPNOTIC TECHNIQUES

Some dream experts suggest using a form of self-hypnosis to stimulate dream recall. This method relies on providing suggestions to your unconscious self, usually in the form of a symbolic action. It seems to be most effective for those who tend to be creatively inclined.

At bedtime, spend several moments relaxing and clearing your mind as much as possible, then offer a direct suggestion associated with tangible symbolism. For example, repeat in your head: "Rubbing my hands together will prepare me to remember my dreams. When I wake, I will rub them together again and recall a dream."

In the morning, lie still and do just as you said, seeing what floats into your mind. This method does not work for everyone, but keep an open mind.

Dream recall is a natural process that will happen easily if you allow it. Building pre-sleep relaxation, affirmations and self-hypnotic techniques into your nightly bedtime ritual can enhance this natural process.

CHANGING YOUR MORNING RITUAL

Once we have established healthy sleep patterns and a bedtime dream recall routine, we then need to work on preventing our mind from running off with the day's agenda as soon as we open our eyes. Worrying about the day's onslaught of responsibilities makes it difficult for the soft voice of dreams to stick in your consciousness. Dreams are not difficult to remember; changing habits to facilitate recall is challenging.

The process of remembering dreams is like meditation in that you adopt a more passive attitude. We allow ourselves to recall dreams rather than force the process. This is nearly antithetical with waking priorities where reason, quick wittedness and achievement demand that we don our persona (the mask we wear to face the world) and adopt the competitiveness often required of waking life.

When you wake in the morning, stay in bed and relax, allowing memories of the night to float to the surface of your mind without judgement or evaluation, as you would a daydream. Take care not to censor any aspect of this experience. When an image or emotion, even the slightest fragment, comes to mind, jot it down in your journal. Sometimes it is helpful to stay in the same physical position for a few moments as you ponder your impressions. Get into the habit of leaving your journal at your bedside so you notice it when you first wake up, and record something daily even if you do not remember any dreams. You can simply note anything you did notice in the night even if it is not a dream. The act of writing is again mentally reinforcing the value of dreamwork.

Some people find that remembering dream emotions is easier than remembering images, at least first thing in the morning, while others find the opposite, and find it easier to remember the images. Bear in mind that some feelings do not translate well to language. Have you ever noticed that if someone asks you what you are feeling it is sometimes hard to put into words? The same holds true for dreaming.

Many new dreamers report that their initial attempts at dream recall feel like a nagging sense that something is there, but they can't remember what it is. Be patient — it only takes a few nights for blurred glimpses to transform into dream fragments and over time to fully detailed dream images and emotions.

Surprisingly, dreams are not difficult to recall. It is unlikely that anyone remembers all of dreams they had the previous night, but the most relevant dreams will come up in no time.

HOW TO JOURNAL YOUR DREAMS

There are some key elements to recording your dreams, especially if you are just starting out working with them. First off, think about your sleeping environment. Do you have a bed partner and, if so, are they receptive to your interest in dreams? This can impact your efforts in a couple of ways. First, if your partner thinks what you are doing is silly you may unconsciously censor your dream recall. Also, do you feel comfortable making the behaviour changes we have discussed in the presence of your partner? If you feel embarrassed or have reservations, naturally this may have an impact.

Novel external stimuli can influence both overall dream recall as well as the dreams we do remember. For example, if you are staying in an uncomfortable hotel room the dreams you remember may have an uncomfortable feel.

It is important to write down your dreams as soon as you wake up as they have an uncanny way of disappearing. A dream journal is personal so there is no one right way to journal. It is likely that your efforts will evolve over time until you find what works best for you. Use the spaces provided in this book to write down your dreams and other journaling information.

Long, detailed dream narratives can be mesmerizing, but are not important for analysing a dream. If you would like to write out your dreams in detail, feel free, then go back and pull out the information discussed here.

An efficient and effective dream journal highlights the critical parts of a dream while retaining the entire narrative's overall integrity. Break a long narrative into brief dream fragments that stand out most. Dream fragments include key images, emotions and thoughts. Use your intuition and pick the one symbol that somehow stands out from the rest. This will be your dream's "primary symbol". Do not worry if it does not seem as visually significant as other objects – dreams do not use waking logic; intuition rather than reason will get you closer to what the dream is saying.

Now do the same for any other images that also seem important but to a lesser degree than your primary symbol. Call these "secondary symbols". You can change these later, but think about your first impressions.

It may be helpful to make a list of words that you feel describe the emotions you experienced. It is likely that many will be interconnected, such as fear, anxiety, nervousness and jitteriness. Circle the one or two that stand out the most. Refer back to the dream map exercise in chapter one. As we noted there, dream feelings can at first feel vague and elusive so jot down anything that will help you describe them.

Jot down any interpretive thoughts and hypotheses that may come to you and that you could expand on later.

You will also want to note basic sleep environmental information if it varies from what is typical for you, such as room temperature, noise, comfort of the bed you are sleeping in, and so on.

Finally, include a section that notes what you are thinking and feeling in the present while recording a dream. Ask yourself: "What am I feeling right now as I write this? What self-statements are going through my mind?" Add this information below your dream entry.

Exercise: How to use a dream journal

Here are some suggestions to get you started with dream journaling, but please customize any of these ideas to fit your needs.

1. Date each entry as you would any journal. Note where you are if you are not in your regular sleeping place or if anything is not part of your normal routine.

2. Note the room conditions (temperature, comfort, light, sound and so on). Any of these veering from what is usual may affect your dreams. Also note your sleeping conditions. Do you use background white noise? It is not a problem if you do the same routine consistently. But if you use it only when you travel, then your dream recall (and dreams) on the road may differ.

3. Note how you are feeling – your mood, fatigue, illness, and so on. You may even want to use a numbered scale (e.g. 1 to 10) to note the intensity of the feeling if that feels relevant for you.

4. As soon as you wake, reflect on the night with as few preconceptions as possible as discussed above. Do you remember anything you felt? Any glimpses of thoughts? Do not look for a full narrative, plot or storyline. A single image or word is a great start. Quickly note any thoughts as they come into your mind. These do not need to be full sentences – use abbreviations, notations, key words, quick doodles and anything to help you quickly capture a bit of the memory before it fades. Longer drawings take more time so these can come later.

5. Break the dream into brief dream fragments as noted above. Choose primary and secondary symbols for each of these fragments based on your intuitive sense.

6. Make a list of words you have used to describe the emotions you experienced. Circle the words that stand out the most.

7. After you have finished, draw a line and below it note what you are feeling right now as you write the entry. What self-statements are going through your mind?

8. Finally, leave space to jot down any additional memories or interpretive thoughts that may come up later.

★★★

Exercise: Remembering dreams with a partner

If you are doing dreamwork with a partner, it may be helpful to create a strategy to remember your dreams together.

1. Sit down with your partner and talk about your desire to remember your dreams. Discuss what it means to each of you and what you both hope to accomplish from your dreamwork.

2. Generate some simple affirmations to stimulate dream recall that feel comfortable to both of you making them as connective as you can. For example, "We are open to our dreams." Use sharing statements rather than I-statements.

3. Quietly take turns repeating the affirmations to one another as you drift off to sleep.

4. When you wake up the following morning, each of you should lie still, keeping yourself in a half-waking, half-sleeping state and let your mind wander. Be alert to any feelings, impressions or images that come to you. Keep your dream journals close by and record these impressions as soon as possible once you are completely awake.

5. Discuss your dreams with your partner. Make your descriptions as vivid as possible, capturing the mood as well as the imagery and narrative. Look for any shared or overlapping symbolism. Ask each other open-ended questions to spark off new thoughts and be sure to offer plenty of encouragement.

Remembering that dreaming is a natural process and changing habits to encourage dream recall provides compelling mental feedback that you are serious about dreaming and will enhance your ability to make productive use of your dreams.

NOTES

_____

_____

_____

_____

_____

_____

_____

_____

_____

_____

_____

_____

_____

_____

_____

CHAPTER

3

WHAT TO DO WITH DREAM INSIGHT

Dreamwork is a window into the unconscious mind offering a rich and unique complement to waking consciousness. It is part intuition and part rationality – two halves of the whole.

Einstein once remarked: "I believe in intuition and inspiration. Imagination is more important than knowledge. For knowledge is limited, whereas imagination embraces the entire world ..."

Think of dreaming as a symbolic representation of waking thoughts containing cognitive, behavioural and emotional components. The goal is to develop self-understanding and then introduce changes in how we think, feel and behave.

There are several dream interpretive methods, all of which have merit, though none of these are perfect for everyone. The final decision on what a dream means always lies with you, the dreamer. As a rule of thumb, insights offered by dreaming will never conflict with waking reason even if they first appear to be at odds. Think of it more as a puzzle to find how the pieces of the psyche fit together rather than a battle for supremacy. It may take courage to accept what a dream is revealing, but once deciphered a dream fits within a framework of consciousness.

Understanding dreams and integrating their meaning into waking life requires nimble cognitive flexibility and imagination. We need to be receptive to our unconscious voice while remaining logical. This will allow us to translate what we hear into our waking world. One of the best ways to facilitate this process is to practise waking imagination. The idea is to nudge us out of the world of pure reason via imagination; as Einstein noted, imagination is enlightening in itself. Here are three exercises intended to build cognitive flexibility and imaginative processes.

Exercise: Imaginative daydreaming

1. Start with an imaginary scene that is familiar and comfortable. This may be a daydream or fantasy you have had before or you can begin from scratch. It should be positive and comforting; steer clear of conflicting feelings. Make the scene as rich in detail as possible, including actions, colours, backgrounds, and so on.

2. In your imagination, act out several versions of the fantasy including what if scenarios to enrich its content. If you imagine seeing a UFO, what would happen if it landed on your rooftop? What if you hitched a ride and hung out with extraterrestrial beings? How would you embellish the scene?

3. Add dialogue if there is none, verbal or extrasensory, and allow all the objects in your fantasy to speak, animate and inanimate – a tree, cat or orbiting planet can all communicate.

4. Create various alternative endings as in some films. Do not be afraid to let your imagination be nonsensical or childlike. The point is to make your imaginative scenes as creative as possible.

★★★

Exercise: Using imagination to develop dreaming skills

1. Find a comfortable, quiet spot, close your eyes and take a few deep breaths. Then begin by a picturing a seed, as small as possible, in your mind. See it hovering in front of you in the air, unaffected by the pull of gravity. Gently turn in all directions; examine it from every angle. Notice its subtle features. It is not perfectly round or uniform. It may first appear to be a solid colour but there is slight variation. It may have a slight texture or indentations.

2. Now mentally change its colour and features, except its size; it is still tiny. If it is dark, lighten it. If it is roundish, elongate it, and so on. Turn it into putty and stretch it, then let it snap back into its original form.

Grow your seed. Keep it floating in midair, but water it (or use any medium you create) to stimulate growth. Notice how the outer hull begins to disintegrate as a tiny sprout pokes out. Make it colourful, then change the colours. All while it is slowly growing and expanding. Keep going until the tiny seed has morphed into a plant with roots, a stem, leaves and any blossoms you care to materialize. Do not be concerned about what kind of seed it is – it can grow into anything you want.

Keep your newly sprouted plant growing and morphing into anything you would like. If you get stuck, start with something you know, such as Jack and the Beanstalk, then morph it into a novel species.

Finally, take a snapshot of your new creation. Hold it in your mind for several moments, then overlay the original seed onto your visualization. At first, this may seem like toggling between images, but keep doing this until the two appear together simultaneously, becoming one life force. This is actually easier to do than to describe.

Exercise: Alternate uses game with a twist

This exercise is an imaginary variation on a commonly performed creativity workshop activity.

1. Sitting at your desk with your eyes open, pick an ordinary object, the first one you notice: computer, mouse, cup, paper clip, book, anything is fine.

2. Visualize the object as it actually is, noticing as much detail as possible. Close your eyes. Slowly begin to mentally transform it into something new and different, even impossible. For example, what if a water bottle was really a spacecraft in disguise? As in the exercise above, maintain a thread of waking logic so that someone else would be able to understand your creation if you explained it.

3. Now pick another object – again the first thing you notice. Stare at this object and repeat what you did in step 2, this time with your eyes open. Squint your eyes slightly to make the object a bit more pliable. It may melt, robotically transform or grow genetically engineered limbs, whatever you wish. This imaginative variation is more difficult than it sounds.

Exercise: People-watching with a twist

Do this exercise in a people-watching spot using the people and their pets that you see to create fantastical storylines. We have all people-watched so the basic instructions are familiar. But the goal here is to creatively transform the watched person into a new or even nonsensical character while retaining sufficient waking logic for the story to be understood. The exercise is done most effectively with a friend.

1. Find a place to sit that has access to a steady stream of people walking by. Pick a person at random. Notice how are they walking — their gait, the kind of clothes they are wearing and so on. Does it fit their appearance? What changes would you make to have them look more humorous, serious or fun? Do they look tired or enthusiastic? If you are doing this exercise with a friend, compare your answers.

2. Create a backstory for each person. Where did they come from? What has their day been like so far? Where are they going and who are they going to see? What is their most deeply guarded secret? What superpowers do they possess? Are they an alien being in disguise? From where in the universe? What would they look like inside

out? Are they displaced in time? Do they dream backward? How would you transform them into a Dali-like painting?

As you can see, the goal has nothing to do with guessing the reality of a person, but it is creative character-building that stimulates your imagination – the more nonsensical, the better.

DREAMS ARE EGOCENTRIC

In dreamwork, the dreamer is always the protagonist. The actions and feelings of your dream characters are only significant insofar as they pertain to you personally. In other words, the dream world may be about places and other people, but those things always represent something connected to you, whether this is your psyche, you in a relationship, you facing the world, etc. Dreamwork is interpreted in the context of your past and present life circumstances.

Consider this dream fragment: "I dreamt I was making love to a rock when suddenly it turned into a rabbit and flew away."

There is nothing irrational about this dream if you remember that waking logic is nonexistent in the dream world. In a dream, making love to a rock is as normal as making love to a person, and rocks can easily turn into flying rabbits.

Dream interpretation is about connecting the dream's feelings and symbols to waking life. Perhaps the dream relates to waking intimacy, such as concerns about a lover who does not attend to your needs and always takes off afterwards. Perhaps it is nonsexual, such as making repeated attempts to establish a connection with a friend who seems to be rebuffing you.

Start with the dream's emotions – what did you actually feel in your dream? This is the dream's epicentre, often its core meaning, and is always the first path to take on your search.

Emotions in waking life can sometimes be misleading, such as when we try to convince ourselves we are happy when we are not. In dreams, we experience the same spectrum of emotions, but these emotions are often literal – joy means joy, sadness means sadness, for example. This is not always the case, but is a safe bet to start your interpretation.

Emotions may be attached to a particular symbol or compose the underlying tenor of the overall dream. Either way, an important interpretive distinction you will be making is if your dream emotions represent situations in your present life or if they are from your past, either the past several years or from your childhood. This can be a challenging distinction as dream interpretation is done through the lens of waking consciousness and this can sometimes block an accurate grasp of feelings.

For example, have you ever felt intensely angry at a friend only to realize that the reason you are angry does not warrant such a strong emotional reaction? It may be that your friend's behaviour has triggered an unconscious memory of being unfairly treated by someone in your past. In this case, the origin of the feeling lies in the past and not with your present-day friend.

Differentiating past versus present feelings is a bit of a dance. There is no simple algorithm to find a solution, but here are some guidelines to follow: in waking life, emotions rooted in the past may feel exaggerated, nagging or physically centred, such as located in your stomach or solar plexus. Dreams indicating past emotions may seem confusing with more incongruous settings or images that appear larger than life, as if viewed from the perspective of a child. You may feel inadequate in the dream, or insignificant.

Dream interpretation becomes more straightforward with practice. As always, if a dream feels unduly distressing or becomes unshakable, processing it with a therapist is always helpful.

CASE STUDY

"I'm sitting in my Intro to Political Science class at college. It's a big room and crammed with students. It looks just like my real class, except the real room is a lot smaller and there aren't that many students. And it smells kinda like schoolboy socks. The professor starts randomly asking questions and the girl behind me always raises her hand fast and always knows the right answer. She's a know-it-all in real life, too. Then my prof looks right at me and asks a question and I have no idea what the answer is. That same annoying girl shoots up her hand, but the prof doesn't go to her — he keeps looking at me. I'm freaking out. I mean I'm really scared. I'm really gonna get in trouble. My mouth gets stuck like I've got a wad of bubblegum stuck in there, not that I'd have anything to say anyway. So I decide to get outta there and pick up my backpack. But I can't lift it; it's like as heavy as lead. Everyone's staring at me and that's it, the dream ends."

Our dreamer is having trouble in college, getting poor grades and dislikes school. He is a musician and that is what he wants to do – play music. There are clues in his dream narrative about where his dream feelings originate:

★ the juvenile quality of the feelings, such as overly intense fear and getting into trouble

★ the size discrepancy between his waking life classroom and the one in his dream

★ bubblegum

★ the scent of boy's socks

★ being powerless to leave the situation (he wants to leave but can't lift his pack)

All of these suggest past emotions so the past may be a good place to begin his inquiry.

INSIGHT FROM DREAMS

Do dreams always offer profound insights about ourselves? Does every dream fragment that we snatch and bring to the light of day truly reflect some aspect of waking life to which we would be wise to pay attention? Most dream workers believe that the lion's share of dreams are meaningful and potentially illuminating, but there are, of course, some dreams that are either incomprehensible or offer little interpretive meaning. In fact, we can overinterpret our dreams, reading significance into every mysterious or intriguing feature. Perhaps certain dreams should be accepted merely as bizarre, if not entertaining, experiences.

If some dreams are meaningful and others are not, how do we tell the difference? Here we go back to the dream feelings again. Complex imagery, vivid symbolism and an intricate plot mean little if a dream feels emotionally static and defies all attempts to seek out a life context. Rest assured – if there is a significant message that your unconscious wishes to communicate and you are receptive, it will return in some form. It will possess a unique feel, even if this is subtle and the images are muddled. Dreams that well up from our innermost concerns always press for attention, either by reoccurring or by nagging at us in the day.

It may be helpful to pay attention to a dream that:

★ is associated with the past, often childhood, even if you do not glean its significance

★ embodies powerful emotions

★ feels unique or out of the ordinary

★ creates feelings that linger well into the day

★ creates impressions or images that are not easily shaken from your mind

★ has a recurring theme, even if it takes on different imagery

While it is certain that we will discover both positive and negative aspects of ourselves in dreams, what happens if we do not like what we find? How do we react if our dreams feel consistently angry and we have regarded ourselves as a non-angry person, or we feel an abundance of confidence in waking life but are scared and helpless while dreaming?

How we consciously view ourselves can be altered by psychological defences. Confusion, denial, repression (memories unconsciously pushed outside of awareness), rationalization, projection (putting your feelings or thoughts onto someone else) and reaction formation (expressing the opposite of one's true feelings) are all common defences that thwart consciousness but that dreams see through. That is not to say a confident person who often feels anxious in a dream is fundamentally insecure. Dreams are meant to be interpreted in context of our life and many factors are at play.

As with anything, the more knowledge we have, the better equipped we are to deal with our challenges. This knowledge may come in complementary forms – reason, emotion, perception, imagination, intuition, dreaming, spirituality or feedback from trusted friends. When a dream features uncharacteristic or disturbing emotions, distinctive symbols or lingering images, it is worthy of note. As always, if a dream feels too disturbing, seek out professional counselling.

CASE STUDY

"I dreamt I was inside Kafka's book, *The Metamorphosis*, where Gregor Samsa wakes up to find he was transformed into a cockroach. I was so ugly. I felt myself crawling, like in the book. I remembered being trapped in his room by my family after the transformation, just like Gregor. I got out of my bed with great effort and tried to get out the door. The door wouldn't open because I couldn't turn the handle. Even though I was enormous, I managed to crawl underneath the door by collapsing my body into a flat blob. I got out of the house and escaped. Then I came across a person walking down the street and called for help. They looked at me disgusted."

In this dream the protagonist sees herself as an ugly, hideous bug. She is confined but manages to escape, but is offered no help and is still not accepted by others. Her calls for help go unanswered.

Our dreamer is creative but stuck. She feels trapped by something that seems unchangeable despite her best efforts. If this was your dream, how would you feel? How would you go about making a connection between the dream symbolism and your life? What would be your next step to try to help yourself?

Exercise: How to interpret a dream

1. Recall your dream and explore its overall emotions, location and timeframe, noticing what stands out the most. If the dream was long and complex, break it into smaller components to allow yourself to take a closer look at each of these parts, their emotions and symbols. These are called dream fragments. There is no harm in doing this since dreams are not time-dependent like a movie.

2. Visualize the dream fragments, trying to recapture as much detail as you can. What is the overall feel or tone of the dream? Try to re-experience the feelings associated with each image.

3. Using your intuition, pick the one image for each fragment that somehow stands out from the rest — your dream's primary symbol. Do not worry if it does

not seem as visually significant as other objects. Remember, dreams do not use waking logic.

4. Ask yourself what you could associate this symbol with in waking life – perhaps something only you would know. Sketch out some connections, either mentally or on paper. Do not worry if what you come up with does not wow you, or if at first you can't come up with anything at all. Dreamwork evolves like peeling layers off an onion. There is no single, definitive meaning.

5. Repeat this same process using other symbols you feel may be important but that somehow stand out less than your primary symbol. These are the dream's secondary symbols. Together these dream symbols and emotions form the core of your interpretation.

6. Try to connect your dream symbols to memories to help clarify their meaning.

7. Finally, what thoughts come to mind right now as you think about your dream. What are you feeling? Look for automatic thoughts – self-statements that just pop into your head, and any associated emotions

CASE STUDY

In this case study, we look at how dreamwork can suggest a practical approach to solving a problem in waking life.

"I have the recurring dream of running a marathon. I start off OK, running most of the way with a good pace, but when I get close to the finishing line, I always seem to get confused and lost. I take a wrong turn or something and can't find the finish line. I keep thinking that I wish I had a map to find the finish line."

Jake chose finish as his primary symbol as this stood out to him the most — being unable to finish the marathon.

For his secondary symbols he chose lost and map.

When Jake explored his dream's emotions, he found that the overall feeling was frustration and that this also came up when HE reflected on all of his dream symbols. He looked for any connections he could make to his waking life and found that the dream seemed to fit his inability to complete projects in a timely manner. He would start a task with confidence and work most of the way through it, but then peter out at the end and either be late or unable to finish. He realized this was a recurring pattern. Jake could not clearly identify his automatic thoughts related to the dream, only that they were muddled.

Jake's dream seems to mirror his waking life, but this does not tell us why he is frequently unable to complete tasks. What the dream did suggest to Jake was that, at the very least, he needed to improve his project organizational skills. Jake needed a map, metaphorically, so he downloaded a time management and organizational app to help stay on track with his projects. The app was helpful and as Jake began completing more projects he felt a growing sense of mastery.

(

CASE STUDY

This case study presents a more complex dream analysis and demonstrates how to break a dream into fragments and analyse each of its components separately.

"The ship was sinking fast. We hit an iceberg and we were going down fast. I remember it was so freezing that the cold made everything blurry. I could tell the front of the boat was already under water because the hull was practically standing up in the water and I was about to slide down the deck. I didn't know anyone because I went alone on the trip. No one wanted to go with me because it was too expensive and they didn't want to spend the money. They told us what to do in an emergency during the prelaunch information session, but this was a vacation boat, not a military vessel. I wasn't really listening. After we hit the iceberg, it was pandemonium. I grabbed a handrail and was holding on for dear life as icy water flooded up the deck. People were screaming as the boat began to submerge into a block of ice. I saw them frozen, not in the water but bouncing turbulently in air over me. I think they got picked off one by one, but I didn't really notice. Then I felt my grip on the handrail start to slip. My hands were freezing and I tried to keep hold of the rail but couldn't. My fingers started to give way. They turned blue, then solid like ice, then cracked like dry ice until only my thumb was left. My hand finally slipped."

The dream is long, but with consistently repeated themes. To make it more manageable, we can first break it up into fragments and take each one at time. But first let us explore the dream emotions. This dreamer reported emotions as global (not tied to a specific dream figure), predominately loneliness, powerlessness and inadequacy, but he felt mostly numb when he woke up.

Fragment 1

"The ship was sinking fast. We hit an iceberg and we were going down fast. I remember it was so freezing that the cold made everything blurry. I could tell the front of boat was already under water because the hull was practically standing up in the water and I was about to slide down the deck."

The dreamer chose freezing as the dream's primary symbol. This may represent a frozen emotional state, keeping emotionally distant from others with the price, of course, being loneliness. The secondary symbol was sinking, which may symbolize losing hope, helplessness and a lack of confidence.

Fragment 2

"I didn't know anyone because I went alone on the trip. No one wanted to go with me because it was too expensive and they didn't want to spend the money."

The dreamer chose alone as the primary symbol and cost as the secondary symbol. Being alone fits with the loneliness theme of the dream, symbolized as no one wanting to join him on his vacation. Note the dream is also pointing out the defensive rationalization (symbolized as cost being the reason no one wanted to join him on the trip), suggesting that the dreamer overuses this defence in waking life. This fragment also provides clues to the dreamer's low self-esteem (he is not worth the money), which reinforces the cycle of rejection and emotional isolation.

Fragment 3

"It was pandemonium. I grabbed a handrail and was holding on for my life as icy water flooded up the deck. People were screaming as the boat began to submerge into a block of ice. I saw them frozen, not in the water, but bouncing turbulently in air over me. I think they got picked off one by one, but I didn't really notice."

Pandemonium was chosen by the dreamer as his primary symbol, which may refer to the unconscious turmoil sitting just beneath the surface of his awareness. He reported no secondary symbols implying uncaring attitude toward his fellow passengers. These images probably do not represent other people in waking life, but rather his own psyche to which he wishes to remain indifferent. This may be an example of a defence mechanism active within the dream suggesting the dreamer is not ready to explore certain aspects of his inner self, and another clue that in waking life he is hiding behind a wall of defences.

Fragment 4

"Then I felt my grip on the handrail start to slip. My hands were freezing and I tried to keep hold of the rail but couldn't. My fingers started to give way; they turned blue, then solid like ice, then cracked like dry ice until only my thumb was left. My hand finally slipped."

The dreamer's chosen primary symbol for this fragment was losing his grip (dream symbols can be actions not just nouns). Here we continue to see his internal struggle being played out and the sense that he is losing the battle to maintain control. He is desperately clinging to the handrail, hoping against hope that he will not have to face his untenable emotional turbulence within.

By working through the dream fragments, we see a theme of internal conflict, overly protective waking defences and the need to confront certain challenging aspects of his psyche. This dream does not reveal what the dreamer needs to face, only that he does need to face something. For this dreamer, it supplied motivation to seek out counselling and explore why he felt lonely and overwhelmed.

NOTES

_____

_____

_____

_____

_____

_____

_____

_____

_____

_____

_____

_____

_____

_____

CHAPTER

4

HOW TO MAKE YOUR DREAMS WORK FOR YOU

Up to this point, we have been discussing what dreams mean and how to interpret them. In this chapter, we will look at ways to consciously encourage dreams to help us facilitate fresh perspectives for approaching life challenges.

DREAM INCUBATION

Dream incubation is a technique to plant a suggestion in your mind at bedtime to address a specific goal. The method uses either affirmations (short mantra-like statements that you repeat to yourself) or a visual image that you imaginatively transform into a goal-directed strategy.

Affirmations should be goal-directed, specific, positive statements that we can repeat to ourselves at bedtime. Here are some examples:

★ I am open to guidance for my decisions.

★ I allow myself to see this situation from different perspectives.

★ I am open to new possibilities to find a solution.

Dream incubation using a visual imagery involves creating a mental image that depicts you mastering the challenge you are facing. You utilize it by focusing on the image you have created at bedtime.

As a loose rule of thumb, visualization may be easier to use for problems that you wish to master while affirmations are more straightforward when requesting guidance from your dreams. However, any image or affirmations you choose are fine as long as they are specific, positive and goal-directed. Intent is the key. Try to approach the task whole-heartedly and with confidence.

CASE STUDY

Emma was the newly married wife of a police officer, having broken her vow that she would never fall in love with a cop. She knew all too well the dangers of her husband's job as her father had been a police officer for 30 years — just before he was about to retire, he was killed in the line of duty. She said no twice when James asked to her to marry him, but he persisted. On the third time he asked, her love for James finally triumphed over her reservations. Unfortunately her anxiety returned early on in their married life as she constantly worried about his job, especially the night shift.

Emma started experiencing panic attacks and frequent nightmares. No matter how hard she tried, she could not shake the feeling that James would not come home. She knew her history of losing her father had a role to play in this worry, but this knowledge did not seem to help.

Emma's dreams were ugly and violent. Her husband, who looked like himself in the dreams, was trapped in a filthy, run-down house with no means of escape and hopelessly surrounded by killers who were about to shoot him.

James was sympathetic to her fears, supportively listening to her as she recounted her dreams and assuring her that such a situation would never happen. Yet the dreams and panic attacks persisted. Emma sought out therapy and also decided to try adjunct dreamwork. She wanted to find out whether her fears represented a legitimate concern for her husband's safety or unresolved emotions from her father's death. She also hoped she could modify the dream's ending so her husband was not killed.

When James was on the nightshift, she would lie in bed visualizing the dream with its newly fantasized ending. She dressed her husband in a magically protective vest rather than his usual bulletproof vest that he wore every work day. This magic vest froze the assailants' bullets in their tracks, Matrix-style. She also used several affirmations, but the one she found most natural was, "I see my husband safe and protected."

After several weeks, Emma had a dream with an unexpected twist:

"I dreamt of my husband; it was not what he looks like, but I know it was him. He was my father from an old picture that was taken before I was born."

In Emma's dream, her husband and father were symbolically fused. This did not surprise her as she knew her fears were connected to her father, but what was surprising was that her dreams began to feel less intense and not as life-like. Over time Emma's panic episodes also diminished in frequency and her anxiety became less disabling.

Naturally Emma's dream does not reduce the risk of James's job, but dreaming was one of the means she used to gain control over her anxiety.

Exercise: Using dreams to solve specific problems

Sometimes it is difficult to deal with a problem because we see no viable options. This exercise will illustrate how to use dreaming to help with money-related worries, although the concept can be applied to a myriad of other challenges as well, from relationships to work-related problems.

1. Take some deep breaths and relax as well as you can, then imagine your money worries as a huge, fire-breathing dragon. The scales on its back are made of bitcoins. Fill in other details with this same imagery until you could describe the dragon to someone and they would get the theme. See the beast clearly in your mind's eye.

2. Now imagine you are holding a humble sword. It is sharp but not large and does not have a jewelled hilt. You also have supernatural speed and can run around the dragon, forcing it to spin around until it is dizzy.

3. As the beast turns, knock bitcoins off its back; this gradually shrinks the dragon in size.

4. Repeat this process until the dragon has shrunk to fit into the palm of your hand. Allow yourself to fall asleep holding the tiny dragon with the realization that it can be tamed – just as your money worries can be overcome.

ASKING QUESTIONS OF A DREAM

Some dream workers believe that a dreamer can pose a specific question before they sleep that their dream can then answer using dream incubation. The method is the same as the one discussed previously except a dreamer asks a specific, clearly phrased question. For example, you may ask, "Should I look for a new job?" or "Should I travel to India?" Naturally your dreams can't tell you the right or wrong thing to do, but they may help to clarify and unpack your feelings on the matter.

CASE STUDY

The following case study illustrates how to ask a question of a dream. It focuses on Emily and Michael, a couple trying to decide if they should become pregnant. The couple vacillated between wanting a child and a reluctancy to lose their freedom. They hoped their dilemma would somehow be resolved but no solution seemed in sight. Their friends suggested that they just go ahead and start a family, advising them that although many couples go through the same uncertainties these are soon resolved once a child is conceived.

However, Emily and Michael were reluctant to follow this counsel. The couple had done some individual dreamwork in the past where Emily had several "baby" dreams, but they had never attempted any cooperative dreamwork. They incubated dreams together, holding hands and asking the question, "Should we have a baby?"

Emily's dreams were first to respond – the image of an empty baby-carrier that in the dream was associated with feelings of sadness. She believed that this dream meant the couple would struggle with regret and emptiness if they decided against having a child.

The couple then used the image of an empty baby-carrier as an incubation stimulus. Emily had a second dream. This time she was running down a narrow, dimly lit street, dodging children who begged her for money as she chased after a missing and ultimately irretrievable clock. Her dream emotions again felt sad. Initially Emily interpreted this dream as a warning of regret, losing this time of their youth if they had a child. But after Michael and Emily discussed the symbolism together, the couple decided it could also represent Emily's biological clock running out.

Emily had a third dream of cuddling and comforting an injured bird that had found its way into a watchmaker's store then flew off to its nest. The couple linked the bird and nest with nurturing a baby. During their incubation exercises, Michael did not have any relevant dreams, but the couple made the decision to go ahead and try for a baby.

When doing shared dreaming it is unusual to have three dreams related to the incubation in relatively rapid succession. However, it is not usual for only one person to contribute a dream that seems to fit the exercise. This does not render the results inaccurate as the person who does not dream can contribute by helping to process their partner's dreams. In this case study, Michael was not as prolific a dreamer as Emily so his lack of dreaming was not unexpected. Note also that the symbol of time presented itself again in Emily's third dream; another sign that the couple thought represented her biological clock.

Exercise: Asking a dream for guidance

This exercise illustrates how to assist you in assertively discussing a disagreement with a friend where tension has escalated beyond the point of differences of opinion, but the guidance could be for any challenge.

1. Visualize a large imaginary house that you live in. The rooms are suffused with your personality, but there is also a spare room for guests.

2. Imagine inviting your friend to stay with you in this house, offering them the spare room and use of all communal spaces.

3. Now imagine what a typical day may be like. What things do they do that may mildly annoy you? For example, being untidy in the kitchen or using a pungent brand of fragrance. Do not include the issue that triggered your differences of opinion.

4. Next imagine the positive things that your friend may do (such as weeding the garden or bringing home takeout) and how that makes you feel about them. Which enjoyable activities would you engage in together, drawing from your memories of before the disagreement?

5. Build up a composite picture of life together in this fantasy house until your visualization leaves you with a good feeling, even with the things that your friend does that annoy you. Remember there was once a time when you forged the friendship based upon caring and mutual respect regardless of differences in attitudes.

6. Let the visualization and the positive feelings stay with you as you drift off to sleep. In the morning note what you are feeling with regard to your friend and look for any images that may allow you to reframe the difficulties you have with them.

CONVERSING WITH YOUR DREAMS

Nearly all of us have thought about a dream we have had, but have you ever considered having a conversation with a dream character? That may sound odd but the results may surprise you. Since dreams live in the world of the unconscious, waking logic does not apply, time and space are irrelevant and, yes, dream figures can converse. And not just animate ones; you can just as easily talk with a tree, a rock or the wind. Naturally we are only talking with ourselves, but perhaps connecting with a deeper part of our mind.

Develop your dialogue in stages from the simplest to the complex. First, accustom yourself to just talking through your dreams, either as internal dialogue or with a friend, noting which symbols seem to catch your attention and, of course, all the associated feelings. Next, begin exploring each of the dream's characters as if you are people-watching. Who do they interact with? Do they speak and, if so, how? What are their mannerisms? What else do you observe? Then, in your imagination, approach one, talk with them and ask them questions. Engage in an open, free dialogue embraced by an attitude of love and acceptance. You are, after all, talking with yourself, perhaps just a mysterious part of yourself.

If you are feeling stuck, some people find it helpful to consult a dream dictionary (or you can try the symbol guide in this book) as a prompt to formulate questions. If your dream character's answers to your questions seem meaningless, do not immediately give up until you are certain a lack of response is not simply because this method feels odd to you. Be sure you are interpreting the answer to the direct question you asked, and not simply your own feelings of discomfort.

Here is an example of a dream that could be conversed with:

"I dreamt about this girl I knew who had passed away. She was really upset. She was crying and I felt like I should be able to make her feel better, but I couldn't. The dream ended with me trying to hug her but not being able to because it felt like there were walls between us."

What would you want to ask this girl? What do you find most curious or triggers the most emotion for you? If she, the dream figure, does not reply in an obvious way, that is fine –

still allow her to participate in the conversation. If what you discover concerns you, talk it over with a therapist or trusted friend.

FREE ASSOCIATION IN DREAMWORK

Free association is a powerful dreamwork technique. It is familiar to everyone – say the first thing that comes to mind, given a particular cue. The idea is to allow the unconscious to generate interpretive directions that otherwise may be blocked by conscious defences.

When successful, the dreamer moves beyond rationally trying to figure out a symbol to generating more creative and unexpected possibilities.

Free association can help you look at dreams in new ways. You may gain insight by uncovering issues hidden from conscious awareness but expressed through symbols.

Exercise: Symbolic free association

1. Before you record the dream itself in your journal, pick an image (object or action) that most draws your attention and write down whichever words come to mind associated with this image.

2. Do not edit your associations. Jot them down as quickly as possible, creating a list of words even if these appear nonsensical. Do not evaluate.

3. When you are done, read over everything you wrote and circle any themes. Look for connections between these themes and your dream and see if you can make any connection to events in your waking life. Look for trends and connections that make sense to you. This exercise can be ongoing and monitored over time to see if a pattern emerges.

USING CALMING SCENTS TO INDUCE A PLEASANT DREAM

The sense of smell has been incredibly useful in survival, so it is no wonder that scents can have a potent effect on our nervous system.

Exercise: Playing with scents

Here is an interesting exercise to harness the power of scent to help induce a calming dream.

Try scenting your bed pillow with a fragrance that you find comforting. The scent you choose can be anything, such as fragrant herbs or essential oils, as long as you find it calming. Do not forget the obvious ones: freshly ground coffee, newly mown grass or citrus fruits.

If you do not wish to use your pillow, you could try an aromatherapy burner as long as it is not overwhelming. You do not want the scent to wake you up. When you wake, note if you feel a greater sense of calm and see if it had any impact on your dreams.

LUCID DREAMING

Lucid dreaming is an extraordinary experience. In essence, it is a state of consciousness where we become aware that we are dreaming while we are dreaming. Lucid dreams are a fascinating hybrid state of consciousness. One can volitionally act on the dreamworld similar to how we act in waking life, except we possess the superpowers that are not unusual in a dream. For example, we can fly, which needless to say can be exhilarating.

Lucid dreaming is sometimes triggered by an event within the dream, such as something that startles us or, for no apparent reason, we simply wake up realizing that we are still dreaming.

"I dreamt I was on the Death Star, creeping across a ledge with a bottomless pit below me, like Luke in the Star Wars movie. I tried not to look down, but I still fell off and I knew I was falling to oblivion. Then suddenly I began to fly. I circled up and hovered next to the platform and looked down."

This is an example of a lucid dream. In this case, the dreamer changes an undesired outcome to something under his control.

How does one induce a lucid dream? This becomes more challenging, and some argue that not everyone can do this. It is possible that lucid dreaming can be induced by becoming more aware of entering a hypnagogic state of consciousness – the transition between wakefulness and sleep. Most people have experienced this state on occasion: that odd feeling where you are not quite awake but also not asleep. Everything feels off and in a state of flux, including sensory perceptions. Paying attention to the onset of the hypnagogic state may train us to "wake up" during a dream.

It is also possible that attempts to induce lucid dreaming are facilitated by receptive pre-sleep attitude.

Exercise: How to lucid dream

1. Affirm to yourself that you are willing to let go of normal reality testing and accept that events or objects are associated with being in a dream.

2. Devise and mentally repeat a positive pre-sleep affirmation that suggests receptiveness to having a lucid dream. You may try something like, "I am open to becoming aware as I dream." Use your own words; intentionality is the key.

3. Look for signs of entering a hypnagogic state. Your waking reality may be morphing, your physical senses may be heightened but at the same feel a bit odd, mental images may be becoming varied and fuzzy, or solid features may start to become rubbery.

4. If you begin to recognize that you are dreaming, try not to startle. This is actually easier said than done. A strong response to the surprise may wake you up.

5. Be patient. For most people, it is rare for lucid dreams to just happen; it takes time and practice. Experiment with different kinds of meditation and affirmations.

DREAM DIALOGUES

A dream dialogue is a conversation with a friend to help you process the meaning of a dream. Your role, as the dreamer, is to present a dream in as much detail as possible remembering that your friend does not have the rich context you possess. You provide as much detail as possible particularly when describing dream images that seem important. For example, if your dream has you zipping through midair astride a cartoon missile that is ready to explode, share what that felt like – scary ... amusing ... exhilarating. Did it remind you of a funny cartoon or video game?

The listener's job is to help process and clarify, not interpret. This is the more challenging role as it requires trying to be aware of and minimizing the projection of their own meaning onto someone else's dream.

Dream dialogues can include free association with the symbols – missile may lead to rocket, launch, speedy or unstoppable; explosion to dynamite, fire, burning, danger or harm. Every dream symbol or emotion can take you to unexpected places. Exploring a dream's ambiguities and paradoxes together may yield some unexpected results.

CO-DREAMING

Co-dreaming is a fascinating technique in which two people's dreams weave together to add insight to both of them. The goal is to build up a composite picture based on both dreams that may be unrelated or similar. You may be wondering if two people can dream the same dream. It is unusual, but it may happen more than we realize.

If we approach this technique as if the unconscious is shared, it does not seem unrealistic. Recall from the first chapter that Jung divided the unconscious mind into two components – the personal unconscious and the collective unconscious – and that the latter houses the collective experience from all people across time. In essence, this is creating a shared consciousness. We can't tap this reservoir of knowledge through conscious awareness, but it may appear in dreams.

Exercise: How to co-dream with a friend

This exercise demonstrates how to use one person's dream to inspire and clarify the symbols of their partner's dream. It takes the form of sharing and interweaving both dreams.

1. Begin with each person choosing a dream they have had recently. Pick dreams that you feel have some overlap, either symbolically, emotionally or simply with an intuitive sense of coherence.

2. You describe your dream in detail as if you are sharing a story, paying particular attention to any symbols that provoked the strongest emotions. Tell your friend which images you chose as the dream's primary and secondary symbols, and why.

3. While listening, your friend tries to absorb the details and nuances of your dream experience. During pauses, your friend may ask open-ended questions such as,"How did you feel ...?" or "Who might the stranger have been?" Keep listening and asking questions until the two of you have built up a composite of the dream's symbols and emotions.

4. Now repeat the same process but with roles reversed: your friend now presents their dream while you listen and question.

5. Now that you have an expanded knowledge of both dreams, look for overlaps or commonalities between them, recalling the reasons why the two of you chose these dreams in the first place. Include symbolic and emotional overlap, not just factual overlap. Notice if anything from one person's dream complements the other's or sheds new light on how to view its symbols. It is helpful to include a shared free association to common elements of the two dreams. For example, if both dreams feature sunflowers this may spark associations such as Van Gogh, art, canvas, cloth, paper, cutting and so on. See where this leads and if it generates any words that feel significant or that increase the overlap between your dreams.

Co-dreaming is a fun and potentially enlightening process. Many people who try this method discover greater insights into their dreams. Some also find that their dreams merge in unexpected ways, particularly dreamers who spend a lot of time together and share many of the same life challenges. For example, one couple discovered that they were both worried that the other was getting bored in the relationship but were too afraid to broach the topic. Two roommates reported that both their dreams reflected concerns about a new tenant who moved in down the hall, though they had not previously shared this information with each other.

DREAM ROLE PLAY

Dream role play is a method of reenacting out a dream with a friend where you both play a part loosely scripted by your dream. The goal is not to act out a long dream, but to transform the dream's uncomfortable elements into something entertaining with overtones of humour that may help to defuse the unpleasant feelings.

The dreamer starts by narrating a whole dream in as much detail as possible – the equivalent of actors giving a play its read through. Then choose your parts. The most obvious approach to casting is for the dreamer to play themselves, no matter what dream form that takes, and the listener to improvise any imaginary figures they can conjure up to counter the threat presented in the dream.

Here is an example using an anxiety dream.

1. 1. First, describe the dream and the feelings it invoked to set the stage.

2. You play the anxious dream character as in the dream. Your partner plays an imaginary figure that provides a defence or counterattack against the dream's destructive anxiety elements. For example, if your dream features a grizzly bear coming out of the woods intent on eating you, your partner may play the role of a gladiator with a huge net to capture the bear or a bee to distract the bear.

3. Now the role play begins. The goal is for your partner to convince your imagination that you no longer have anything to fear. You, the dreamer, can ask what if questions, that your partner must try to foil. For example, "What if the bear eats the gladiator, then comes after me?" Your partner, as the gladiator, may reply that he turned into a bee that stung the bear on the nose, making him run in circles. "What if the bear swallows the bee?" The bee flew down the bear's intestines and emerges at his butt and stings him, making him dance a jig.

4. Turning anxiety into humour may to help defuse distressing feelings. If the same images reappear in a dream, these may feel more muted.

NOTES

_____

_____

_____

_____

_____

_____

_____

_____

_____

_____

_____

_____

_____

_____

CHAPTER

5

EMOTIONS IN THE DREAM WORLD

After we wake from a dream, odd or quirky images can quickly grab our attention. But dreams erupt with emotions. They may be subtle, intense or exaggerated and are often an expression of how we really feel in waking life.

Interestingly, most research suggests that dreams tend to be emotionally polarized, either mostly negative or mostly positive, rather than neutral. From an interpretive point of view, these dream emotions forge a map to our innermost selves providing insight into how we face daily concerns, fears and desires. Some dream feelings replicate how we feel in waking life – for example, sadness, joy or anxiety. However, other less apparent emotions such as fear and guilt can be more confusing.

Dream emotions can linger but not always distinctly; some are experienced as a vague feeling in the body or as a hollowness carried throughout the day. When this happens, it is time to take notice and probe what the feeling may mean. In this chapter, we will explore some of the most common dream emotions, where they may come from, and practical ways to use dreaming to improve your waking emotional state.

ANXIETY, FEAR AND PANIC

Everyone has experienced anxiety in waking life and nearly everyone has done so in a dream as well. Waking anxiety can be acute, chronic or sometimes lead to full-blown panic attacks, but regardless of how and why it manifests we find it in dreaming. Sometimes anxiety dreams may serve as a kind of catharsis deescalating emotional overflow in waking life. At other times dream anxiety can feel exaggerated – a clue that we may be overlooking these feelings in waking life.

Let us say that one night you dream of being thrown into a dungeon and left with no food or water, and that the following week you have a dream in which you are flying in a plane and discover there is no one in the pilot's seat. The dreams have different content but both are saturated with feelings of panic. Is your inner voice shouting to pay attention to what may be bubbling beneath the conscious surface?

When you record your dreams, spend some time focusing on any associations that these feelings may have with important aspects of waking life. Have you noticed an underlying worry, however subtle, that may be nagging at you? For example, did you overhear a supervisor describing a coworker in a way that made you realize you are beginning to see them as a rival?

A common feature of anxiety dreams is threat — being chased, falling in terror, being hunted and helpless to defend yourself. The famous horror movie theme of running down a hallway that keeps getting longer and longer is inspired by dreams. Dream characters can feel dangerous or unfriendly. As always, if you find your dream feelings too distressing, speak with a therapist.

Exercise: Creating an animal avatar to overcome fear

If you are facing a fearful life situation, why not invite a dream guide to help you explore your inner strengths to confront this fear? Dream guides are hidden skills that we all possess but may be buried beneath layers of insecurities. We can use these to boost our confidence and promote creative thinking. One way to identify a dream guide is to imbue an animal avatar with a fear-conquering skill, then incubate your dreams with this chosen creature.

1. Choose an animal that you wish to represent your dream guide. The choice may be straightforward, such as a lion for courage, but it does not need to be. For example, you may choose a tiny mouse to represent stealth and the ability to find its way into any situation; a gazelle, speed and grace; an owl, wisdom; a horse, loyalty and intelligence; a snake, the ability to strike fear in an adversary; or an eagle, which soars above the ground viewing the world from many different perspectives.

2. Each night before you drift off to sleep, meditate on your chosen animal, concentrating on the skill you wish to harness. Imagine yourself entering a world where you, as your animal avatar, have conquered fear and can move freely without fear.

3. In the morning, review your dreams looking for associations with your animal avatar (if not the animal itself). Look for symbolism. If your avatar was a turtle, did its protective shell provide feelings of safety? If it was a fox, did you notice its clever strategizing? Did your avatar bird soar above the mundane and offer any new perspectives?

4. How did the dream itself feel? What automatic thoughts came into your mind? And did your dream offer wisdom, food for thought or suggestions?

GRIEF AND SADNESS

Dreams play a role in helping us cope with grief and sadness. These dreams usually have a quality of helplessness to them.

Sadness and grief may be associated with more frequent dreams of negative mood, nightmares and more helpless or passive dream characters.

Sometimes dream feelings surprise us and are not what they seem to be. Sadness can be one such dream emotion. Feeling sad in a dream may reflect sadness in waking life. This is straightforward, easy to spot and fits what we know about our current life situation. But dreams of joy may also compensate for when we are overwhelmed by sadness while awake, such as when we are going through times of intense grief. Dreams help to regulate the balance of our psyche, so when we tip too far in one direction our dreams bring us back closer to equilibrium. This is called a compensatory dream – restoring some kind of balance to our psyche.

"I recently lost my husband and was plagued with fits of crying spells every day. Then I had the strangest dream. I dreamt I was by the ocean. It was a clear, beautiful day: calm and serene. I felt the water surrounding me even though I wasn't wet in the ocean – I was standing on the beach. The water felt warm and comforting, and I was overtaken by a profound sense of peace."

This is a dream of compensation – dreams infused with feelings that are the opposite of what the grief-stricken person was experiencing in waking life. Dreams of compensation provide a temporary cushion, a psychic balance, when we need them most. As the grieving process progresses in waking life, compensation dreams begin to fade.

If you are struggling with excessive sadness, grief or depression, it is always wise to consult a therapist.

ANGER

Anger is often a secondary emotion, meaning it covers another feeling that is more painful for us to experience. For example, it is usually easier to feel angry than it is to feel helpless so we unconsciously cover our vulnerability with anger.

Anger that is displaced is also not uncommon, meaning we believe we are angry for one reason (usually something about someone else) when in fact it has nothing to do with this target but stems from something about us that we are disinclined to acknowledge. Road rage directed at another driver would be an example, as would anger-fused bigotry and hatred. Out of fear, we heatedly blame others under the false belief that they are responsible for our problems.

Coping with anger in dreams is similar to the methods we use in waking life — learning to accurately understand our feelings and practising anger-incompatible behaviours such as meditation, relaxation and self-talk. Cathartic approaches to anger have been found to be ineffective and in the long run only begets more anger. For example, punching a pillow or punching bag may release energy and feel good temporarily but it does little to solve an anger issue.

Even if anger is justified, dreams can help to diffuse the feelings. Try using the next exercise to help calm angry feelings. Our goal is not to generate a calming dream, though this can happen, but to find a calm, peaceful waking state of mind to fall asleep in and to wake refreshed with a peaceful loving attitude.

Exercise: Creating a calm state of mind to help overcome angry feelings

1. At bedtime, use one of the dream incubation strategies described above to prime your dreams. Positive affirmations or calming images are both helpful, whichever you find most comfortable. Affirmations may include:

   ★ I seek a state of calm, peace and compassion.

   ★ I allow feelings of peacefulness to flow through my body.

   ★ I am free from judgemental attitudes.

2. If you prefer to incubate your dreams with an image, choose one that does not evoke negative thoughts or angry feelings. The image should leave you with a sense of calm and peace. The specific visual aspects of the image can be anything as long as it is infused with a peaceful aura.

3. When you wake, notice how you feel. We are not looking for a specific dream but for a peaceful state of mind. Do a body scan to see if you are carrying tension anywhere in your body. What thoughts are popping into your mind and what is the emotional valence of those thoughts (that is, are they negative, positive or neutral)? Practise nightly until you are able to fall asleep and wake in a calm state of mind.

SPIRITUALITY AND SERENITY

Some dream workers report increases in wellbeing if spiritual insight is introduced as the focus of dreamwork. They believe that many spiritually oriented dreams feel serene and embody spirituality in whatever context that means for an individual. In some dream systems, certain symbols represent spirituality – for example, water, sacred icons and forgiveness.

Spiritual dreaming shifts the focus away from the challenges of daily life to a sense of something bigger than ourselves. The dream emotions may be carried over into the day offering a perspective that seems less mundane. Unfortunately this heightened state of being tends to get lost in the stress of the day.

Spiritual dreams do not solve specific problems or offer unique solutions. Instead they feel deeper, more ethereal, transcending and timeless. Many spiritual leaders suggest their purpose is to help clarify our values, discover connection and beauty, and facilitate a search for deep personal meaning. They may also impact daily life by softening attitudes and enriching a sense of wellbeing.

Exercise: Cultivating spiritual dreams

1. Incubate your dreams by creating mantra-like affirmations that request spiritual clarity and guidance. Here are some example affirmations:

   ★ I allow my spiritual unconscious to emerge in my dreams.

   ★ I allow myself a connection with my soul.

   ★ I am open to my higher self.

2. Use your own words, keeping the message positive and uplifting. Remember that you are not seeking a specific answer or asking for a miracle, but you are looking to connect with your deepest self or, if you prefer, something larger than you.

3. When you wake, lay still and focus on what you feel more than any specific dream image. You are not intending to translate symbolism into rational thought, but to embrace the experience.

GUILT AND SHAME

Guilt is one of the most misunderstood emotions in life. It may feel intimidating but it is usually a valuable emotion with a purpose to remind us that we have made a mistake and guide us to either do something about it if we can or to try to do a better job in the future.

Guilt is often mistaken for shame, a destructive emotion that feels similar but is not the same. Shame is a self-chastising attack that we launch against ourselves based on conditioning from our past. The key difference is "I did something wrong", which we all do, versus "I am a bad person".

Take these three examples:

1. André felt bad because he knew that he was putting his career before time spent with his family. He was torn between the two. When feelings of guilt began cropping up more frequently in his dreams, he began to think more seriously about how he could balance his professional and home lives.

2. Blair was becoming increasingly uncomfortable with his parents dropping hints that they wanted him to lend money to his brother who was recently unemployed, even though the brothers hardly saw each other. At first Blair thought his parents were nagging, but he reconsidered when he had a dream that reminded him of fond childhood memories with his brother.

3. Cecilia loved her job and deeply wanted to move her career forward, but was always too timid to volunteer strategic ideas to her supervisor. She watched as others spoke up, and found they were the ones getting promoted. She dreamt she was confronted by her mother who chastised her for something she did not do, but as soon as she tried to speak up and defend herself, Cecilia suddenly felt embarrassed and fearful and said nothing. After processing her dream with a friend, Cecilia realized that her fear was not about work but was about her mother who endlessly criticized her choices, sending the message that her ideas were never good enough. The dream prompted Cecilia to take more risks at work and increased her willingness to offer ideas that may be rejected.

How can you spot the difference between guilt and shame in a dream? There are several signs to look for:

★ How do you feel toward whichever symbol is representing you in the dream?

★ Does the dream prompt you to look at the mistake you made with an eye to improving yourself (guilt)? Or does it leave you with a sense of hopelessness (shame)?

★ Are the dream feelings associated with a sense of pervasive inadequacy (shame) or a mistake or shortcoming (guilt)?

★ Does this feeling frequent your dreams often or bring up old memories, often from childhood (shame)?

★ Do you feel the dream was prompted by something you have regretted doing recently and would like to improve (guilt)?

Shame can be tricky and degrade our quality of life so it is often wise to sort it out with the help of a therapist.

INSECURITY AND NEEDINESS

We all feel insecure and needy from time to time. Both extroverts and introverts are dependent upon others for emotional nourishment: sometimes we desire warmth, closeness, understanding, companionship or simply the company of another person.

When we are missing personal and professional relationships that meet these needs, our energy, consciously or not, often focuses on searching for one. Sometimes these needs are obvious to us, but they may also be obscured by psychological defences, particularly if we think of ourselves as strong and independent. If overly zealous defences are in play, we may consciously experience a vague sense of dissatisfaction or emptiness, but nothing more concrete. Either way, these needs will appear in dreams.

Struggling with chronic feelings of insecurity or neediness is usually reflected in dreaming. These dreams may vary in frequency from occasional to near nightly if we are in the middle of struggling with a relationship.

Dream images may present with a combination of positive and negative imagery but will feel insecure or needy. There may be something that is missing in the dream, searching for something or yearning for a connection while seeing other dream characters making connections. These dreams sometimes feel lonely or even mildly panicky.

Dreamwork may help to muster the inner resources necessary to cope with these unpleasant feelings and help boost self-esteem. At bedtime, meditate on feelings of confidence using self-statements that affirm your strengths. These should be qualities that you truly believe are positive about yourself, not something you are trying to convince yourself of. More general self-affirming statements are also useful, such as, "My true self is limitless," or "I find strength and harmony in myself." Another technique is to meditate on a symbolic image that represents your positive self before you sleep – perhaps as an agile bird or a solid, healthy tree.

Exercise: Using dreams to build self-confidence and decrease neediness

All of us are afflicted by bouts of self-doubt and sometimes too readily blame ourselves for errors we think we may have committed. The following dream incubation exercise is designed to bolster self-esteem.

1. Before you drift off to sleep, imagine a box that contains three objects that you prize. These do not need to possess monetary value and should not pose emotional conflicts (such as an heirloom that reminds you of grief). Visualize each object in turn: let us just say for the sake of example, an old drawing, a ring or a coin. Identify qualities in yourself that you may associate with each of these objects. The drawing represents your creative side, the ring is commitment, and the coin symbolizes personal growth. Remember that these are just examples, so choose anything that fits for you. Keep the visualization alive until you find yourself drifting off to sleep.

2. When you wake, notice if any dreams relate to your visualization. What automatic thoughts come to mind? Over time you may find this unconsciously strengthens your confidence in waking reality.

Exercise: Visualize releasing your resentment

Everyone experiences resentment from time to time, but when this feeling insidiously blossoms it will show up in a dream. Resentments store up grievances, alter our perceptions to focus only on the negative, and magnify annoyances out of proportion. Needless to say, resentfulness can harm all aspects of life, especially relationships, not to mention making us feel drained. It takes energy to stay resentful all the time.

Dreamwork may offer an antidote to resentment. Here is an imaginative exercise to try.

1. As you drift off to sleep, and as close to the hypnagogic state as you can get (the place between waking and sleeping), visualize tiny bubbles rising out of your head toward the ceiling.

2. Within each bubble is an image representing resentment. Watch as it floats gently upward and disappears through the ceiling.

CASE STUDY

"I was walking along the shore of this lake and spotted an old classmate from college. I had not stayed in touch but read that he had done well in life, got rich, had a big house in the city and married the beautiful woman from school I always wanted to get to know but could not. I was broke and divorced and had just lost my job, which was not much of a job anyway. I felt stuck in a dead-end loop. I was beginning to feel depressed and hopeless."

The dreamer harboured feelings of resentment in waking life, not just toward former college classmates but also toward others around him whom he saw as more successful. When he woke from his dream, it struck him that the feeling of hopelessness in the dream was exaggerated. He was not actually divorced — in fact, he was content in his marriage. He had not lost his job, and his career was not stuck. In this case, the dream seemed to be a reminder of what he had in his life, to not look back, and helped to motivate him to move forward.

NIGHTMARES

The most extreme emotional experience in dreaming is a nightmare. They are terrifying and compelling as you feel real, palpable fear. Characters may take the form of surrealistic monsters or a person who seems threatening. We are usually convinced in the dream that something tragic will happen.

Why do we dream of being chased by a stranger with an axe or falling off a cliff? What is it about the nightmares where everything seems out of control and the more we try to fix it the more impossible the situation becomes? There is no universally accepted answer, but we know that almost everyone has experienced at least one nightmare and that these can result from stress, depression or physical pain. Nightmares can be induced by medicines or triggered by traumatic memories or considered idiopathic, which simply means that they are unique to the individual with no identifiable cause.

It is not unusual for a dreamer to describe a nightmare as a premonition. They may feel anticipatory as if a tragic event is lurking. Some psychologists suggest that the prophetic meaning we attach to a nightmare comes from our attempts to connect meaning to the experience.

Nightmare symbolism can be broken down into two themes:

1. the experiences of being overwhelmed

2. that of being confronted by something menacing

Naturally these can manifest in many different ways. The former of these include dreams of drowning, becoming frozen or being in a room closing in. In the latter, we may be being chased by ominous figures or chasms are about to swallow us up. Either way, we are left feeling helplessness and vulnerable.

Some dream researchers suggest that distressing dreams are the psyches' way of coping with daily stress. We become actors in a dream world, creating ways to work through problems that we face in waking life. Another possibility is that nightmares are unconscious warnings that we are stretched too thin, sinking in stress. This is a frog boiling in water idea – we do not notice the mounting stress until it becomes so overwhelming that our unconscious alerts us.

There is no true universal cure for nightmares, and reducing their intensity or frequency depends largely on the cause. It may be helpful to track them in a dream journal so that you can be sure of their actual frequency. Reducing stress, maintaining good sleep hygiene and monitoring which media you consume in the evening may be of benefit. There are also some medicines you can discuss with your doctor. As with any psychological symptoms, consult a therapist if you feel troubled.

Finally the age-old question: does a distressing nightmare of dying mean you are about to die in waking life? The answer to this is simply: no, it does not.

CASE STUDY

The following case study illustrates the use of directed imagination similar to the techniques we discussed in chapter four to help reduce the distress of a recurring nightmare. This can be done on our own or with the help of a trusted friend.

"I dreamt Lucas was captured by the monster and disappeared right before I got to him. I saw the monster and it was horrible with sharp teeth and slimy skin. I didn't see exactly what happened to Lucas but I remember thinking he was frozen and then teleported away. I felt devastated I couldn't help him. I know it sounds ridiculous but these nightmares seem real and almost always wake me up in the middle of the night."

Kimberly's nightmare involves her partner, Lucas. He is paralyzed, then disappears and is presumably killed (though she never sees this) by a hideous monster. She experiences feelings of guilt for not being able to save her partner.

Kimberly and Lucas work together to help with Kimberly's nightmare by reimagining the dream together, then verbally acting it out with improvised alternative positive endings. Kimberly sets the stage and Lucas contributes so that the entire made-up dream scenario becomes interactive between the two of them.

In one imaginative scenario, Kimberly keeps chasing the monster, but when Lucas feels the paralysis is about to set in he yells at the creature. This distracts the monster, giving Kimberly the opportunity to sneak up on it and disable it with a phaser before it can teleport Lucas away.

Kimberly's goal was not to interpret the meaning of the dream but to find ways to lessen its distressing impact. The couple used directed imagination, a form of role play designed to make someone feel a greater sense of mastery and control. They created several imaginative scenarios using the dream's structure and elements but with improvised positive endings. The value of the repetition was not to find the right fantasy but to help ease the distress provoked by the nightmares via repeated exposure.

Several approaches can be used to treat distressing dreams. These include cognitive behavioural therapy (CBT), relaxation, medicines and exposure therapy. Always seek out a therapist if you find your nightmares worrisome.

Engaging directed imagination is a process similar to those we discussed in chapter four, but here is a simple template.

★ If you are doing this on your own, start by getting comfortable, relax and close your eyes.

★ Imagine yourself in whichever challenging situation concerns you by picturing as many elements of the scene as you can.

★ Allow the scene to passively flow before your eyes as if you are watching a movie.

★ When you come across the point where you would like to gain more control, take on a more active role.

★ Switch up the scene any way you wish as long as it feels safe and never introduces harm to yourself or others.

★ Play it out until you feel a sense of mastery over the events of the daydream.

It is sometimes even more effective to do this with a friend as long as you feel safe and comfortable with them as you can brainstorm different scenarios that you may not think of on your own. Use the same approach as above, except play it out in a more role-play format just as Kimberly did with her dream. Imagination is an amazingly potent tool.

NOTES

_____

_____

_____

_____

_____

_____

_____

_____

_____

_____

_____

_____

_____

_____

CHAPTER

6

DREAMS AND
RELATIONSHIPS

Relationships benefit enormously from dreamwork. To begin with, dreams offer heightened self-understanding, and it is impossible to relate well to others if we barely know ourselves. Dreaming gives us a clearer view into the heart of a relationship. It allows us to disclose our true feelings and express our aspirations of what we want for ourselves and our partner, friend or family member.

In this chapter we will explore how dreamwork can enlighten relationships of all kinds, from coworkers to friends and family to an intimate partner to long-term commitment. We learn how dreams clarify our feelings and sharpen our intuition so that we can make healthy relationship choices, and how dreams aid communication with our partner at every crucial stage.

In intimate relationships dreams provide a unique opportunity to work with your partner to face challenges. The wisdom of dreams teaches us to understand and define our own needs better, as well as to gain a deeper appreciation of those of our lover. We will explore how sharing our dreams with our partner can open a mutually reinforcing dialogue, and we will examine how dreams can provide unexpected insights into the relationship breaking down emotional barriers. You can do several exercises with your partner, ranging from the purely playful to the more psychologically challenging. These are all designed to build on the existing strengths of a relationship and help you work through the inevitable weaknesses.

CASE STUDY

Paul never paid much attention to his dreams until he and his wife, Sofie, began to drift apart after 17 years of marriage. Their problems had built up so gradually that they were hardly noticeable. There were no real fights: superficially they still seemed to get along well, handling minor crises together without contention, but the passion that once filled their relationship was slowly fading. Neither felt the intimacy they once had, and sex became unsatisfying for both. When Paul was promoted at work, he celebrated with friends; Sofie did not learn about his promotion until the next day.

Sofie began feeling increasingly empty. It was as if she and her husband were no longer the friends and lovers they once were but instead were becoming two people keeping house together. She tried to discuss her feelings with Paul but he thought she was overreacting, especially when she asked if he was having an affair. Sofie's parents also rebuffed her concerns. She was told that no marriage is perfect and that she ought to be thankful for what she had. With nowhere to turn, Sofie felt as if her spirit were slowly being drained away.

Then Paul had a dream.

"I saw Sofie leaving home by herself to go hiking into the mountains in the middle of winter. Although I thought it odd that she would go alone and in such cold conditions, I didn't pay too much attention. Weeks, maybe even months, passed and she never returned home. I began frantically talking about the trip to everyone I could find: people I knew, strangers, animals, even the snow. No one seemed concerned, except the snow, which didn't answer — it just kept falling. I thought about going up to the mountains to look for her, but I was too busy at work and hanging out with friends, so I never got around to it. Instead, I tried to brush aside the idea that something bad had happened to her. Then I saw a woman lying face down in the snow on the street. She didn't look anything like my wife, but somehow I knew she was and I knew that if I did not help her immediately, she would die."

Paul woke from the dream in a cold sweat. He did not immediately understand his dream, but found it odd that what struck him most was not the image of the woman who he knew was his wife but it was the snow. He sat up in bed and looked over at Sofie who was sound asleep. Then it came to him. He remembered a souvenir snow globe that the couple had brought back from a wonderful vacation they had taken in Paris years before – a model of the Eiffel Tower encased in plastic that stirred up a blizzard when you shook it. The souvenir was long gone but its memory triggered a deep nostalgia and Paul suddenly realized the meaning of the dream – he needed to stop taking his marriage for granted or he would lose it. Paul related his dream to his wife and the couple decided to attend counselling together to help them rebuild the relationship they had once shared.

INTIMACY IN DREAMS

The esteemed psychologist Erik Erikson once described intimacy as the ability to fuse our identity with someone else without fear of losing ourselves. Relationships with friends, family, lovers and colleagues offer the opportunity to help us define our individuality and discover new and wonderful things about ourselves.

Intimacy in dreams manifests in many ways. Some dream images may seem obvious, such as touch or intertwined symbols, but do not be lured by what appears to be common sense. Remember, common sense is a product of waking reality. A lonely dream figure in the distance may also represent intimacy if the dreams overflows with feelings of connection.

As with all dreamwork, explore your dream feelings. If a dream reflects unconditional feelings of attachment, it may be a dream of intimacy.

OVERCOMING FEAR OF INTIMACY

A common obstacle to building intimacy is fear. A relationship may begin to feel claustrophobic, as though walls are closing in and our individuality is about to be smothered.

As with many troubling feelings, dreams reflect what we truly feel, uncensored by conscious awareness. Symbols of entrapment and enclosure, sometimes quite literally like walls closing in, or being stuck underneath a sheet of ice and being unable to break through, may all represent feelings that are being stifled. More abstractly, we may find that our identity in a dream has merged with that of someone else, such as looking into a mirror and seeing another face that we know is us. Dream symbols are intensely personal so what you experience may well be different from what someone else would give a similar predicament. Always look for the dream's overall emotional tone as a guide.

Of course relationship claustrophobia can be very real in waking life. Someone with a dominating ego may sadly have an agenda to suppress our growth, intentionally or otherwise. And there are occasions when this sense of emotional suffocation is less reflective of the relationship that we are in than of our own fears.

To boost your self-confidence, at bedtime consciously modify troubling dream symbols in your imagination before falling asleep. For example, imagine looking in the mirror and seeing a confident image of you being reflected back. Or imagine yourself bolstered with self-confidence and behaving more assertively with the intimidating person.

ATTRACTION

Have you ever asked yourself why are you attracted to someone? The answer lies deeper than physical appearance, shared interests or humour. The mysterious alchemy of attraction resides in the unconscious, usually based on early formative experiences. The old adage that we marry our father or mother has some merit, if oversimplified.

As mentioned earlier, a recognizable dream image is usually not a literal representation of the actual person in waking life but is a symbolic clue to the nature of what draws you to a potential partner. Does the dream image that represents the person of your attraction feel natural, comfortable and inevitable? Are the symbols infused with feelings of kindness and connection?

For example, the dream image of a tree attracting a flock of happy, colourful birds may represent trust or a sign of connection. Piece together fragments from different dreams that may have a connection with the person of your attraction – scenes, settings, characters, emotions – and see what composite you discover. Using your imagination, engage in dialogue with your dream characters – what would they say? Ask questions such as: "How does a dream character feel about the nature of your relationship?" If this may seem odd, remember that imagination gets us closer to our unconscious mind. Explore the symbol guide at the end of this book, not as a definitive explanation of dream symbols but as a thoughtful tool of exploration.

ROMANTIC RELATIONSHIPS

Relationships are remarkably complex – balancing careers, making decisions about children, accommodating our partner's needs, and countless other challenges that are part of having a committed relationship. The reality is that it is impossible to be in a serious relationship and not take the other person's needs into account in nearly all the decisions we make.

Do we want to make the sacrifices necessary to share our life with someone? This is a decision that should be made both consciously and unconsciously. Waking consciousness is encumbered by defences that can influence our decision-making. For example, we may convince ourselves that we are freely choosing to remain unpartnered when in reality we are avoiding a relationship because we fear intimacy.

Naturally, dreams can't pick a partner but they may help us to navigate our conscious defences.

Exercise: Choosing a partner

This is a common workshop exercise that helps to translate psychological subtleties into colours that may offer some clarity about attraction.

1. Choose a set of colours and give them meanings. For example:

★ **blue** – creative, emotional, cerebral or remote

★ **red** – passionate, fiery, driven or unpredictable

★ **green** – logical, connective, compulsive or jealous

★ **gold** – wise, determined or uncompromising

★ **orange** – warm, courageous or elusive

★ **violet** – intuitive, spiritual or dreamy

★ **brown** – earthy or practical

★ **black** – mysterious, powerful or alluring

The colours themselves are arbitrary, so choose ones that feel meaningful to you.

2. Next consider which three colours best characterize your personality, following the attributes you have chosen. Then based on whichever palette you have created, consider which colours would most complement your own and supply the qualities that you lack – these symbolize your ideal partner.

3. Weave the colours of your potential partner into a dream incubation. Each night before you fall asleep, set the scene by visualizing the setting, figures and objects you wish to appear. For example, if you are seeking someone represented by blue, imagine symbols of the sky or water. If you would prefer a person with green characteristics, imagine lush landscapes or gardens, and so on.

4. Finally, see what comes up in your dream, particularly your dream feelings, about someone you regard as a potential partner.

A commonly asked question is, "Can dreams tell me if I'm in love?" If someone is phrasing this question as they may phrase a tarot reading, then the answer, of course, is no. But dreams may help us to recognize when we are overly idealizing a love interest, confusing love with neediness or are afraid of intimacy.

Exercise: Nurturing a relationship

Relationships require attention and can never be taken for granted. Try the following dream inoculation to seed your unconscious with intention to keep a relationship thriving.

1. As you fall asleep, visualize your relationship as a beautiful garden. Recall how this garden cast a spell on you – how you first tilled the soil, planted the seeds and nurtured their growth.

2. Picture yourself in your garden and feel its features: intimacy, the exquisite flowers, commitment and the perennials you have planted that return each year. Visualize how you nurtured its growth by weeding out problems, strengthening it by sharing and companionship, and supporting one another by being strong when your partner is struggling.

3. If you experience literal dreams of growth – nature, landscape, nurturing, water, paths, trees or flowers – consider how these may be interpreted in light of your relationship.

EROTIC DREAMS

Sexuality overflows in dreams. Sociological surveys find that most of us have experienced at least one erotic dream and that many people have these dreams regularly. Erotic dreams appear to be universal, occurring in all cultures, across genders and throughout the lifespan.

Why does sex feature so prominently in our dreams? The short answer is that it is because it features prominently in waking life. The longer answer is more complicated, including the assertion by some psychological traditions that libido encompasses far more than carnal desire. Libido represents all life energy – vitality, instincts, motivation, creativity and just about every way we approach our world. Obviously such monumental energy is bound to be represented in dreams.

In addition to being plentiful, erotic dreams are misunderstood. This may be because of how we interpret them. Many people tend to take them literally or feel their imagery is uncomfortable. In actuality, erotic dreams are not intended to be threatening and are rarely literal. For example, a dream of making love to our best friend's partner may make us uncomfortable but it does not mean we want to do this in waking reality. Sexual dreams, just like all dreaming, are primarily symbolic so their meaning could be almost anything depending on us, the dreamer.

The bottom line is that erotic dreams should never be a source of embarrassment or fear. Instead, they should be treated and understood no differently to nonsexual dreams. In addition, dreams that do not contain any obvious erotic images may refer to sexuality. Psychoanalysts sometimes interpret some dreams as having disguised sexual content – famously, apples or peaches represent breasts, the act of climbing a ladder suggests sexual intercourse, and an airplane references male genitalia.

Let us explore some possible hypotheses about the meaning of erotic dreaming, bearing in mind that no one can interpret a dream but the dreamer.

1. Erotic dreams may afford a healthy way of releasing sexual energy. It is possible that erotic dreams provide a safe outlet when this energy is not being adequately expressed elsewhere. There is some evidence that celibacy triggers more frequent sexual dreams.

2. Erotic dreams may be a barometer of the quality of a relationship at any given time. For example, if we feel that we are not receiving enough emotional nourishment, sexual dreams may conspicuously lack warmth or affection. We may go through the motions of making love in a dream but feel nothing, or we may have sexual dreams that feel hollow.

3. Erotic dreams may have more to do with energy and creativity than sex. Any consideration of sex in dreams can't overlook these alternative explanations.

4. Finally, sexual dreams that feel positive may simply be enjoyed and not interpreted. They can be unpredictable, fun and safe. There is nothing to fear from feeling excited by images that depict you doing something you would not necessarily do while awake, and they do not mean that you have an unconscious desire to act out this fantasy.

RELATIONSHIP CONFLICTS

Conflicts are inevitable in any relationship. How can two human beings with distinct personalities, separate histories, competing needs and differing attitudes and opinions not have differences from time to time? Obviously having a disagreement does not mean that the relationship will devolve into a disaster, or even close to one. All healthy couples have disagreements but they find constructive ways to resolve their differences.

Dreams of conflict in a relationship may express anger or frustration, though not necessarily at your partner. They may be about your professional life, about frustrations with yourself or a prompt for you to act more assertively in some matter. Conflict dreams may allow a dreamer to confront a threat in a safe manner – the opportunity to "practise" a response to an intimidating challenge you are facing in life. When we fail to make headway on a problem, the conflict may arise in dreams to help provide a fresh perspective and a constructive way forward.

CASE STUDY

Everyone noticed Jason and Tara's volatile relationship. They always looked either madly in love or were yelling at each other. They admitted it as well, but they also acknowledged that they felt a deep connection. The couple could never just talk. Their interactions burst with emotion, whether joy or anger, whenever they tried to discuss anything of consequence, and even more mundane conversations could become confrontational as each battled for control. Predictably, following every argument there was an equally intense reconciliation when sex and intimacy knew no bounds.

Aware of the emotional toll on their marriage, Jason and Tara decided to address the turbulence in their relationship. The couple had heard that dreamwork might help them to understand their tumultuous relationship, and both wondered if their personalities were incompatible. They were both prolific dreamers and began to keep dream journals. To neither's surprise, each reported wildly vivid dreams, usually emotionally charged and often sexual. When they compared their journals, they discovered that their dream frequency, intensity and thematic content seemed similar. The couple took this to mean that they connected at a deep level.

The couple tried repeating affirmations each night to stimulate dreams of cooperation instead of aggression. Holding hands before they went to sleep, each quietly described a setting that felt peaceful and soothing – tranquil waters and gentle cooling breezes. Gradually their dreams progressed to more harmonious imagery and emotions including symbols of mutual support. One of Tara's dreams was of the couple rowing a boat together with their oar strokes perfectly synchronized.

Over time Jason and Tara's daily life became calmer and their dreams less aggressive. The couple began to recognize power struggles before they got out of control and learnt to tame their competitiveness and become more mutually supportive.

Exercise: Summoning the strength to reconnect after a conflict

How do we reconnect with someone after a conflict? This dream incubation exercise is designed to soften hardened feelings that may linger or turn to stubbornness.

1. At bedtime, relax, take a few deep breaths and clear your mind as best as possible.

2. When you feel relaxed, visualize yourself floating against a calming blue background. Imagine yourself at peace as a beautiful light that emanates from within bathes you in its radiant aura. Feel the warmth and serenity that the light brings.

3. Visualize your friend floating next to you. Imagine that they asked to join you and try to sense their presence. They are also at peace and surrounded by light.

4. When the image stabilizes and feels comforting, imagine that the two of you slowly move closer together until the two auras coalesce as one. Allow yourself to drift off to sleep in a content state.

UNDERSTANDING DREAM JEALOUSY

Jealousy is a primitive and fearful emotion. Many of us are reluctant to admit that we feel jealous, but nearly everyone has experienced this feeling both in waking life and in dreams. Jealousy often has a primal quality and comes up easily in dreams, particularly if we fear an assault on our self-worth or struggle with abandonment issues.

Dreams may help us to understand if jealous feeling are concerns about our present relationship or if they stem from a past emotional injury. For example, dreaming of catching our partner flirting with someone may represent a concern or suspicion or may reflect past fears. Naturally, dreamwork can't tell us what our partner is up to but it may prompt us to rationally evaluate the situation.

Sometimes jealousy dreams stem from a loss. For example, a partner breaking up with us may trigger a jealousy dream if we see somebody happily attached, even if we do not know them.

Exercise: Understanding and coping with jealousy

1. When you wake from a dream with jealous feelings, think about the overall dream drama. What happened in the dream? How did the various dream characters relate to each other? How did those interactions feel?

2. Identify a dream character that you feel is associated with your feelings of jealousy.

3. Reflect on what you know about this dream character. What is it about them that makes you think they represent jealousy? Since dream characters usually symbolize parts of ourselves, consider what this may represent within your own psyche. Could this be a reminder of being hurt in the past by an ex-partner? Do the dream feelings remind you of abandonment issues? As always, use your dream emotions as a guide.

PAST LOVERS THAT IMPACT PRESENT RELATIONSHIPS

Sometimes the shadow of a former lover falls over our relationship, making us feel like we do not measure up. This can lead to the trap of comparing ourselves with a ghostly rival. We may agonize over simple mistakes, hold grudges, feel paranoid or lash out in anger, then be overcome with regret and fear.

Dreams of possessiveness and hoarding may reflect this retrospective jealousy. For example, we may dream of our partner being out of reach – perhaps on the other side of a chasm or in a different building glimpsed only through a window. Dreams of inadequacy or feeling trapped are common.

Unless there is waking evidence for your concerns, such as your partner being flirtatious with their past lover, incubating dreams for self-esteem building may help. Self-esteem is not just defining who we are; it is about how we feel about ourselves. It is affected by how we see ourselves relative to the world around us, including the past, which can sometimes seem bigger than life. Dream incubation is usually best if it is present-focused even if we are struggling with past events, such as our partner's ex.

Exercise: Making peace with the past

1. Begin by identifying positive attributes about yourself — what makes you unique and special? Do this independent of your relationship.

2. Develop a set of affirmations that affirm you and celebrate your strengths. Be sure to phrase them in a whole-hearted, self-affirming way. For example, if you believe humour to be one of your strengths, you may use the affirmation, "I am fun and enjoyable to be with." Avoid an affirmation such as, "I am usually funny," which places limits on yourself.

3. You may also use affirmations that make peace with the past, letting go of ghosts. Again these affirmations should be positive and present-focused, such as, "I live in the present."

If you feel you can't make peace with the past, talking with a therapist or trusted friend can also be helpful.

INFIDELITY

Most psychologists view infidelity as a breach of trust, not just a sexual indiscretion that can leave a lasting mark on a relationship. It can trigger feelings of inadequacy while awake and in dreams. If the relationship is to survive, trust must be rebuilt. This rarely happens automatically – time does not heal all wounds; healing requires hard work from both partners and sometimes professional guidance.

Needless to say, infidelity often elicits powerful dream emotions. Dreaming can't tell you about your partner but it can help to clarify your own feelings. It will not help to ask a dream if your partner is cheating. In some cases infidelity dreams symbolize dissatisfaction with the current state of a relationship, such as a desire for more time with your partner or, conversely, more alone time. These dreams may reflect something about yourself independent of the relationship.

Exercise: Understanding the meaning of infidelity dreams

1. Is the dream loaded with unpleasant feelings accompanied by thoughts or symbols of betrayal, suspicion or dishonesty? Do you truly suspect your partner of cheating? If so, why? Have you spoken with your partner about your concerns? If not, why? Have you spoken with a friend or someone with an unbiased opinion of your partner?

2. Could the dream be hinting at an emotional or nonsexual intimacy problem within the relationship?

3. Is there a place in your relationship where you need to be honest with yourself? Are you being true to yourself, not just sexually but in any aspect? Are you acting according to your beliefs and values?

4. Could the dream have nothing to do with infidelity but suggest confusion or uncertainty about a choice you need to make or a desire for support in overcoming adversity?

DREAMING ABOUT AN EX

Dreaming about an ex-partner is common and can be recurrent. Some people report these dreams when they have yet to get over their ex, but these dreams may also reveal inner anxieties about themselves. There are many questions you may ask yourself. You can also look for clues in the dream.

★ What is the emotional tone and content of the dream?

★ What are your memories of this person?

★ Are you reminiscing about time spent together?

★ Is there a longing in the dream to rekindle a relationship with your ex?

Are you idealizing the good parts of the relationship and minimizing the bad?

Ask yourself if these feelings could be arising from loneliness or whether this is a true desire to be with this person again. Consider the reasons and context of why the breakup happened in the first place. Remember that when we are lonely familiarity feels comforting.

Also consider these following points.

1. How do the dream figures communicate? Clearly and effectively with understanding? Or is it confusing? How does this relate to what you recall from your relationship with your ex?

2. We always learn something from relationships regardless of how they end. Does this dream remind you of unresolved problems you are working on?

3. Are you struggling with moving on from this relationship? Do you struggle with abandonment issues (these are far more common than most people realize)?

DREAMS OF REJECTION

"I dreamt that my partner and I got into a fight and we broke up. I guess I should say he broke us up. In the dream we were both calm and collected throughout the entire thing, which made it worse, because all I felt on the inside was numb. The dream ended when he walked away from me and I was left alone in a parking lot."

The images may differ but many people report having had a dream with this theme. Dreams of rejection are often triggered by an event in waking life but may also precipitate past experiences and childhood feelings of rejection. Dreamwork can offer a safe haven for building self-esteem.

Exercise: Using dream incubation to ease feelings of rejection

1. At bedtime, settle in by closing your eyes and taking some slow, diaphragmatic breathing.

2. Imagine you are seeing someone whose company you enjoy, where you feel comfortable and safe and they are clearly returning your affection. Visualize the fantasy down in detail (such as where you go, what you are wearing, who else is there, and so on). Stay with the image until you feel comfortable and secure.

3. Let yourself drift off to sleep. Watch for any negative self-statements that may sneak in, such as "It can't happen" or "They are going to reject me". Remember that this is your fantasy so it can be whatever you wish.

4. When you wake in the morning, jot down whatever comes to mind in your dream journal. As always, do not give up after a few attempts; dream incubation takes time.

CASE STUDY

Bethany's breakup with her partner was unexpected and unwanted. She did not see it coming when he broke the news. He did not leave room for discussion or seeing a couple's therapist. In his mind the relationship was over.

After he left, Bethany lost faith in relationships, herself and others, resulting in several years of being alone. She continually tried to reassure herself that she did not need anyone, that she was perfectly happy on her own and that she was not lonely. She had supportive friends, a satisfying job and newfound freedom to do as she pleased. She often glanced at the wiry wood plank she hung in her apartment that read: "A woman needs a man like a fish needs a bicycle."

However, over time Bethany's denial waned. She was lonely. She wanted a partner. She was tired of casual, uncommitted sex. Unfortunately she still found trusting someone to be a challenge.

She read a book on dreamwork and decided to try a dream incubation aimed at re-establishing what she believed was impossible – love. At bedtime Bethany repeated a simple affirmation mantra: "I can walk on clouds." She chose this affirmation for its metaphorical value – to believe again in something that she felt was impossible. It took several weeks but one night she had the following dream.

"I stood gripping the head of a lion gargoyle atop the Notre Dame Cathedral in Paris. I looked out over the city then closed my eyes, held my breath and slowly stepped out into midair. What happened surprised me, even in the dream, but I guess not enough to wake me up. I didn't fall. I was suspended in the air. At first I was a little scared but not that much. I just contentedly watched the city bustling below, then gently floated to the ground."

The dream invigorated Bethany, making her feel more alive, and was the turning point in her restored hope for the future. She entered therapy and began working through the challenges to her beliefs about herself and others.

ENDING A RELATIONSHIP

Few experiences are as emotionally taxing as ending a relationship. Even when it is our decision to make that call, the situation is usually challenging and of course we would always want to be mindful of the other person's feelings. Dreams can bolster our strength and guide us through a compassionate breakup.

Dreams are uniquely personal but can also help us to see things from a different perspective. Learning about ourselves helps us to interact with others, even in challenging situations, helping us to act responsibly and with compassion. In short, we may imagine difficult scenarios and how we could handle them.

Here is a dream incubation that may help the process of ending a relationship.

At bedtime, create a mindful visualization seeing yourself having a conversation with your partner about breaking up.

★ How would you phrase what you want to say?

★ What would be the kindest way to approach your partner?

★ See yourself as calm and caring but assertive.

★ Speak from a place of kindness toward yourself and your former partner.

Use affirmations to that embody love, clarity and wisdom: "I seek the wisdom to recognize my path; I seek love and compassion for others; I seek the strength to persevere on my path."

Finally, a separate dream incubation may address how to handle the aftermath. This may include a willingness to do some self-reflection about the part you played in the relationship not going as you would have liked, and what you can do within yourself to facilitate growth and learning.

WORKPLACE DREAMS

Most of us spend more time at our jobs than we do anywhere else. For many of us, work is not just our livelihood but is our primary source of identity and self-esteem. Work also presents some of our most challenging relationships. We usually do not choose our coworkers or the politics of the workplace. It is no wonder that stress and conflicts emerge. This, of course, will be translated in dreams.

As you might imagine, work-related dreams take many forms depending on the stressors that are most prominent for the dreamer. Competitiveness and ambition may feature symbols of jealously or struggles, feel urgent or combative, or trigger childhood feelings of sibling competition. Themes of failure, frustration, judgement, fear, helplessness, communication and inadequacy are common. We may even experience dreams of retribution, which are certainly healthier than suppressing such emotions or acting them out in waking life.

(

CASE STUDY

"I dreamt I woke up from dozing off in my office cubicle. I was sitting on top of my desk, the size of a pencil sharpener. I realized that I was tiny and screamed for help, but nobody heard my voice over the office din. I started asking everything on the desk for help: a stack of papers taller than me, a plant and an organizer. Maybe they could suggest a way to get me back to my real size? But when I asked my computer, it just glared at me. Then it attacked. It started chasing me across the desk and finally backed me up against the edge. It was charging at me. I knew it was going to knock me off and that the fall would kill me. I woke up terrified, this time for real in my bed."

The dream was set at work in the dreamer's actual cubicle, and he interpreted it to be about his job. He was recently passed over for promotion and was feeling stressed and worried. He did have difficulty completing a critical report, largely because his company had installed a new software system that he was not able to master. He reached out to coworkers for help but they were unresponsive, symbolized in the dream as no one hearing his pleas for help.

The dream presents intense feelings of worry, powerlessness and inadequacy. Unfortunately the dreamer was forced into early retirement, something his intuition did not miss. He did receive an unexpected severance package that allowed him the opportunity to enter therapy to reduce his overall stress level before seeking a new job.

SHARED DAYDREAMING

Nearly everyone daydreams. Our mind may spontaneously drift off at work or in the classroom – at any time or anywhere. These waking fantasies span the entire range of human experience, from planning daily responsibilities to adventurous escapes and romantic encounters.

Daydreams fall within a state of awareness that psychologists call a differentiated waking state. This is somewhere between active consciousness and sleep. Most of us have experienced the intensely colourful images and exaggerated sense of reality that can occur in a daydream, similar to the transition from sleep to wakefulness known as hypnopompic hallucinations. The most interesting feature of daydreaming is that it is under our direct control.

Daydreaming can also be a mutual exercise in which two people can daydream together where both contribute to a shared experience by exploring themes of shared interest. The kernel of the fantasy may come from either person, but the unfolding process is mutual and spontaneous. Both partners contribute to the free flow to create a winding progression of images, twisting and turning in unpredictable ways and, to an extent, governed by the unconscious mind. As the daydream evolves, both project unconscious material into the fantasy to reveal feelings and attitudes that may have been previously hidden from awareness.

You can also manipulate a daydream through a process analogous to lucid dreaming. For example, if your fantasy comes to a halt or you feel vulnerable, take control of the daydream and deliberately develop the characters or plot in such a way that brings about a more positive outcome. Afterwards, process the story you developed with your friend as if it were an actual dream.

Exercise: How to share a daydream with a friend

Daydreams offer a glimpse into the unconscious way that a projective test (such as Rorschach Inkblot) can reveal parts of ourselves that we are not consciously aware of. This exercise shows how to share and build your daydreams with a trusted friend. It is important to do this exercise with someone you wholly trust because the process can be unexpected and revealing.

1. You start off by setting the opening scene: setting, time, characters, and so on. For example, if you are off to the future, what is the time frame? The near future? A thousand years off? You fill in any specifics you wish to include.

2. Your friend then expands on what you have created by adding their own elements, prompting a deeper exploration of the daydream. Build the fantasy together so that it feels right for both of you. Continue the process with as little censoring as possible. Let your imaginations run wild as if you are creating a surrealistic painting together. For example, your story may begin in ancient Greece where you are standing on Mount Olympus with the god Zeus and looking down on Earth. Your friend may ask what you see. Your reply may be: "Tiny people that look like ants walking around – they remind me of people walking on the street below my office." Your friend may add that one of these people started to fly like Superman. You may add that your ants make you feel like you are a worker drone at the office and the flying ones make you think of escaping your job.

3. As the story evolves, both of you share your associations pertaining to yourselves, your

aspirations, and so on – whatever comes up for you. Ask each other questions relating parts of the story to your daily lives. The results may surprise you.

FAMILY CONFLICTS

Every family experiences conflict and like all emotionally charged themes these conflicts are likely to appear in dreams. Generally, dreams of family tend to fall into two categories.

★ External conflicts arise from stressors outside the family unit, such as one member's work stress that overflows via anger or a lowered tolerance to frustration.

★ Internal conflicts are arguments or rivalries within the family, such as siblings arguing or parent-child issues.

Dreams associated with family problems are similar to those of other conflict sources – a noticeable emotional manifestation, then personalized symbols. Symbols of jealousy, rivalry, frustration and helplessness are all relevant here. Family is a unique set of relationships in that we do not choose our family nor can we easily discard them, even if we think they are dysfunctional.

CASE STUDY

Dylan sought out therapy after he experienced a startling dream. He had been struggling to cope with his defiant 12-year-old stepson. He was getting easily frustrated, overreacting, quick to punish and blocking all communication with the boy. What Dylan found most frustrating was that he could see the mistakes he was making almost as soon as he made them and instantly regretted what he had done. Yet he could not stop falling into the same patterns over and over.

"I don't remember much of my dream. It was fuzzy; I couldn't see anything clearly. I just know I was in the counsellor's office when I was 12. My parents sent me. I remember my dad always saying, 'Liz is better than you. Why can't you be more like your sister?' He would say that all the time. But I woke up thinking about it in the middle of night and put it together – that's just what I'm doing to my stepson!"

Dylan's insight flowed out of a fuzzy dream with unrecognizable images. Parents often repeat the same pattern of behaviour they were subjected to as a child, usually around the same age. Fortunately Dylan's dream provided insight and strong motivation to work on his childhood history as well as his relationship with his stepson.

DREAM TELEPATHY

Dream telepathy refers to a form of remote communication between two people, one of whom is in a dream state of consciousness. It is analogous to waking telepathy (communicating with someone else psychically). Dream telepathy is more than merely having a dream about a friend; it is willfully communicating with them while they are dreaming. As you may imagine, this is a controversial topic.

Early experiments took place decades ago. The most extensive of these was the famous Maimonides project, named for the New York hospital where a series of experiments were conducted. Here is the basic methodology that was used at Maimonides:

1. A person sleeping in a dream laboratory at the hospital (the receiver) was monitored by EEG. This EEG alerted the researchers when they were likely to be dreaming.

2. At the EEG alert, another person (the sender) was awake in a separate room and would mentally concentrate on sending a predetermined message to the dreamer, who did not know the contents of this message.

3. The following morning, the receiver was shown a series of pictures and asked to rank them according to the likelihood that the pictures related to the message sent by the sender.

Several studies were conducted at Maimonides. Most demonstrated statistically significant results. The receiver correctly identified images corresponding to what the sender had been imagining. However, subsequent studies done elsewhere failed to replicate these results and both the original research as well as the replicating studies have been the subject of debate.

Whether or not dream telepathy is possible is unknown, but if you want to try this with a friend, the exercise below shows a fun way to go about it.

Exercise: using dream telepathy

1. Your friend is assigned as the dreamer and goes to sleep at a predetermined time.

2. About an hour after the scheduled sleep time (when dreaming is likely to occur), you physically act out a message, rather than just imagining it. For example, you jog on the spot, dance, skip with a rope or vigorously wave. Do not tell your friend ahead of time what you are planning to do.

3. The next day, check with your friend. If they noticed a dream, ask them to describe what they saw and see if it is similar to the movements in your message.

NOTES

CHAPTER

7

GUIDED DAYDREAMING

Guided daydreaming is a method to actively explore the process of dream interpretation using daydream scenarios. A daydream, consciously constructed by you or a friend, substitutes for an actual dream and offers practice in thinking through the process of interpretation.

This chapter presents four daydreams. Each daydream is followed by expressed or implied emotions and some possible questions to ask about the narrative. Imagine each one as a dream you may want to understand.

Guided daydreaming may also serve as a form of dream incubation. Try thinking through these as if they were an actual dream.

A SHIP ON STORMY SEAS:
a guided daydream to help cope with fear or embarrassment

A sailing ship enters turbulent waters and is tossed about on the waves so roughly that it is in danger of sinking. The crew are terrified by the ferocity of the storm and look to the captain to save them from this life-threatening ordeal. But the captain dithers. He has never faced such a dramatic situation before and is unsure what to do for the best. Fearful and guilt-ridden, he hides away in his quarters as the crew bang at the door, begging for direction and a plan that will save their lives.

EMOTIONS

Fear

Guilt

Embarrassment

QUESTIONS TO ASK

★ What does the dream storm feel like to you?

★ Do you, as captain, feel isolated and alone?

★ Why do you feel so incapable of making a decision?

★ Do you believe that the ship will sink if you do not act decisively?

★ Why do you feel safer in your cabin than on deck?

★ Should you, as a crew member, take action on your own without the captain's consent? If not, why?

★ Are there lifeboats on board?

★ If so, are you able to reach them?

★ If the crew were to abandon ship, would you follow? If so, how would this make you feel?

THE VASE AND THE DOVE:
a guided daydream to explore our inner emotional complexity

A man and a woman are arguing. The man wants to spend a month travelling alone – a long-held ambition. As they argue, the man backs into a table, which prompts a precious vase, an heirloom belonging to the woman, to fall to the floor and shatter. The couple break off arguing when they notice an oval object on the floor rolling away from the shattered pieces of the vase. The man bends down to pick it up. It is an egg. As he holds it, the egg hatches and a tiny dove emerges, fanning out its tail as it nestles in the palm of his hand.

EMOTIONS

Anger

Loss

Jealousy

Surprise

QUESTIONS TO ASK

★ What might the vase represent?

★ How do you feel when it breaks?

★ What is your reaction when you first see the egg?

★ What might this dream egg represent for you?

★ What connection do you make between the vase breaking and the egg you have discovered?

★ Do you see travelling as a metaphor? If so, for what? Ambition?

★ What do you think is the significance of the dove?

★ How do you feel when you first see the dove?

★ Why is the dove so small yet so powerful?

★ Where will the dove fly to when it takes wing?

GIBBERISH, GESTURES AND DRAWINGS IN THE SAND:
a guided daydream for better communication

At first she thinks she is alone on the remote island but she soon discovers that someone else is there. This is a total stranger whose language and methods of communication are completely foreign. The stranger tries desperately to communicate, talking loudly and frantically, but fails. They also try to gesture and draw in the sand but all to no avail.

EMOTIONS

Confusion

Frustration

Inadequacy

Helplessness

Feeling frantic

QUESTIONS TO ASK

★ Which characteristic of yourself do you see in the woman inhabiting the remote island? The stranger?

★ Do you feel safe there?

★ Is the stranger a friendly figure or do they feel potentially threatening?

★ What are the characteristics of the stranger's language?

★ Is this language more or less expressive than your own?

★ Why do you think the stranger is so frantic to communicate with you?

★ Why do you find it so difficult to understand the stranger's language?

★ What symbols does the figure draw in the sand?

★ If you had to make a guess about the message the stranger is trying to convey, what would it be?

THE DEPARTING TRAIN:
a guided daydream to come to terms with loss

Two lovers are standing on the platform of a train station as the steam engine moves up the tracks. One of them is ready to leave. They kiss goodbye and one watches as the other mingles with the crowd that is climbing aboard the train. The one left on the platform waves, but only to a fog of steam as the train slowly pulls away from the station. They stand there feeling lonely and lost, surrounded by the general commotion of the station carrying on as normal.

EMOTIONS

Loss

Loneliness

Sorrow

Abandonment

Neediness

Grief

QUESTIONS TO ASK

★ What did the lovers' kiss goodbye at the station feel like?

★ Which one of the lovers do you most identify with?

★ Where is the departing lover going and will they be coming back?

★ If they will be back, how long will they be away?

★ What are your thoughts as their train pulls out of the station?

★ What are the feelings of loss and loneliness for the partner on the platform?

★ What is the other person's feeling?

★ Why is the crowd so uncaring?

CHAPTER

8

THE DREAM
SYMBOL GUIDE

Throughout this book we have emphasized that dream emotions are the key to deciphering the language of dreams. However, dream images are rich in symbolism with unique interpretive value for each individual.

This symbol guide provides an alphabetical directory of some key symbols presented in dreams and brief interpretive descriptions intended as a thoughtful starting point for developing your own personalized analysis. The suggestions here can't tell you what a dream means but they may prompt creative associations.

Be open-minded and question what is written here. Change or expand each definition in the context of your dreams, emotions and waking life circumstances.

ABANDONMENT

Loss or disappointment

Were you the abandoned or the abandoner? Has someone close recently let you down and, if so, who? Were you let down by a parent in your childhood? Do you feel that you have not been fully committed to your current relationship?

ACTOR

Self-consciousness

Perhaps you are prone to focusing too much on outward appearances (your own or someone close to you), or you are too concerned about another's point of view when you make decisions about yourself. Do you feel that you are under close scrutiny from someone close? Have you been judgemental of someone (with or without their knowledge)? Are you and a close friend or partner overly competitive?

ALIEN

Isolation or disconnectedness

Are you confronting an unfamiliar aspect of a relationship? Have you or a friend or partner changed direction recently – perhaps on an issue or in your career? Are any major decisions looming, such as moving house or beginning a family?

ARMOUR

Defensiveness

Could you be shielding your true feelings from someone close? Do you feel particularly insecure about a certain aspect of your relationship? Are you feeling pushed down an avenue you would rather not take – perhaps at work rather than at home?

AURA

Insight, understanding or protection

How might your partner or closest friend need your help? What unresolved issues in your relationship require one or other of you to be more perceptive? Do you feel safe in your most important relationships?

BELL

Unconscious messages or warning of impending argument

Were the bells in your dream hand bells or church bells? What things do you know deep down to be true but have brushed aside in waking life? What concerns have you and your partner discussed but perhaps left unresolved?

BOAT

The course of a relationship

In your dream was the boat cruising gently or being tossed about by waves? Do you feel that your relationship is steering the right course or headed for turbulent waters? Do you feel in control of the relationship?

BODY

Supportiveness and inner strength

In your dream were the images of the body strong or weak? In life do you feel that you have a healthy support network among your friends? How supportive are you of your partner, and he or she of you? How do you express your support?

BRIDGE

Friendship

In your dream did you cross the bridge or were you stranded on one side? Was the bridge robust or flimsy? Are there friendships that you feel need attention? Which steps could you take to cultivate these relationships? Do you have any anxieties about your ability to make friends?

BUILDING

Related to you, your partner or the relationship

The entire edifice may signify a relationship while each room is one of its many facets. What kind of building was in your dream? How might its architecture reflect your relationship? For example, a warehouse may represent holding on to old attitudes or a castle may suggest hopes and aspirations.

BULL

Sexuality, competitiveness, temptation or stubbornness

How did the bull appear in your dream – calmly grazing or ready to charge? How might its actions (or inactions) reflect the tempo of your sexual relationships? Is it that your partner is unmoved on an issue important to you or are you being stubborn?

CHASING

Conflict or escape; elusive goals

Were you being chased or the chaser? Were you chasing a person or something intangible? What difficulties are you facing – at work, at home or among your friends?

CLEANING

Emotional cleansing

What was being cleaned in your dream? Do you feel the waking need to communicate more openly with your partner? Are there unresolved issues that need your attention?

CLOCK

Maturing relationship, sexuality or urgency

Look at the metaphor. Are you aware of time running out? Is someone putting pressure on you to make a decision or get something done? Where would you place your current relationship if it was a stage in life (such as childhood, teenage years, twenties, and so on)?

CRACKS

Change, transforming attitudes or conflict

How precious to you was the broken item? Was it repaired or swept away? How has your relationship matured over the past months? Has anyone close to you done anything to make you question their friendship? Which relationship issues might you be ignoring rather than fixing?

CROWN

Superiority, authority or control

Did you identify with this symbol? Did it feel powerful or authoritative, perhaps overly so? Was there any sense of helplessness associated with this dream? Do you feel that you control your relationship or that you are controlled? Are there specific (unresolved) issues with figures of authority at work or at home?

DEATH

Transformation (death is rarely meant literally)

Who died in the dream? Did your dream self feel release or anguish at the death? Are you and your partner trying to set aside old differences and move onward? Could there be issues of the relationship's direction to tackle? How do you view its future and does this coincide with your partner's view?

DOG

Security, loyalty, attention-seeking or control

In what ways do you feel vulnerable or unprotected in your relationship? Does the dream-dog's loyalty seem to represent your own or your partner's real-life commitment? Was the dog well-behaved or disobedient?

FALLING

Feeling out of control, fear, helplessness, threat or letting go

Falling may be dreams of control that represent a need to feel that we are not helpless or faced with circumstances that we have no control over. These dreams may occur when we feel especially stressed or overwhelmed and without a clear direction on how to cope with something that seems to be becoming increasingly unbearable. Stressors that may trigger dreams of falling may be obvious or subtle. Ask yourself if you feel like you are running out of options in tackling a particular problem, say, at work or in a relationship. When you think of this issue, does it bring up feelings of anxiety or helplessness?

FATHER

Strength, authority, protection or problem-solving; dominance, sexual power or aggression

Whose father appeared in the dream? Did the figure bear any likeness to your own father or anyone else you know? Was the figure gentle or aggressive? Do you feel that this dream represented your relationship with your family or your partner? If your partner, do you have issues about authority within the relationship?

FESTIVAL

Compensation or good news; fear of evaluation or exposure; being lost in a crowd

What was the mood of the festival in the dream? Were you revelling among the throng or trying to escape the commotion? Who, known to you, was with you? In waking life, are you harnessing any particular secrets for which you fear exposure, perhaps with friends or at work? Do you feel that your voice is unheard within a relationship?

FLYING

Coping with insecurity; freedom, achievement or growth; sometimes a prelude to a lucid dream

Flying is a common and universal dream symbol. The act of flying can take on many forms from gliding on top of wind currents like a bird to laboriously swimming through air. Some dream workers believe that flying dreams that feel free, buoyant and invigorating are representative of spirituality — a search of discovery, inspiration, transcending the mundane. Others suggest flying is associated with imagination — viewing life from new perspectives. Did the dream feel alive and invigorating? It is possible these dreams may reflect a liberation from responsibilities or stressors? Have you recently been wondering about a deeper meaning of life?

GIFT

Desires, needs or friendship

Did you give or receive the gift in the dream? Who was the giver/recipient if it was not you? Was the gift given in kindness? How was it wrapped? In waking life, how do you approach new friendships? Do you feel the need to make an offering to put a relationship back on course? If the giver was known to you but not a family member or partner, could the person have hidden qualities?

HEART

Nurture, comfort or unconditional love

In the dream did the heart appear symbolically or literally – perhaps as a heart-shaped vase? If literally, what was the item made from? In waking life do you feel secure in your love for your partner and family or unsettled? If you have just embarked upon a new relationship, could the heart represent your blossoming feelings for your new partner? Or could it be a warning that you are moving too quickly?

ISLAND

Isolation, misunderstanding or illicit desire

Did your dream self feel lonely or relieved to be on an island? Were you trying to reach somewhere else? Was anyone else with you? Is there something that you want to tell your partner but can't find the words to articulate? Do you feel that your partner has left you behind in some way? If the isolation is welcome, are you feeling trapped by circumstances?

MAP

Change, direction or charting a course

Did you follow the map in your dream? What was it directing you to? If in waking life you have marked out goals within your relationship, could the map be showing you the way toward them? If the map was hard to follow, is one particular goal proving more difficult than you first expected? Which changes in direction could benefit a relationship?

MARRIAGE

Companionship or working together

Was the marriage your own? If not, whose? Was the bride or groom your partner? Are you and your partner successfully working through difficulties? Have you and a friend or partner recently embarked on a common course that previously presented difficulties? How secure do you feel in your relationships?

MAZE

Confusion or indecision

Who was lost in the maze? Were they able to find their way out? Did the person seek help to escape? What could be found at the blind turnings? What was in the centre and at the exit? In real life are you and your partner undecided about something?

MOTHER

Nurturing, spiritual beauty, purity, the giver of life, aloofness, jealousy, manipulativeness, control or protectiveness

Did your dream reveal a personal symbol of your mother or an archetypal representation? How did she behave toward you? What was she wearing? How did your dream self feel about the figure?

MOUNTAIN

Hope or aspirations; daunting tasks

How did you feel when you saw the mountain? Were you at the bottom or at the top or somewhere in between? Was your partner there with you — by your side or elsewhere on the mountain? If you were at the top or partway up, what could you see below you? How have you and your partner determined to improve your relationship? Could the mountain or your positions on it represent how you both might get on at achieving those aims?

NUDITY

Exposure or vulnerability

Who was naked in your dream? Was it a single character among a crowd of clothed people? How did the nudity make you feel? Did the dream figure try to cover up or hide? What were the other dream characters' reactions? In waking life have you let slip something you would rather have kept hidden, perhaps from a friend, work colleague or partner? How could this indiscretion impact on your relationships with people concerned? Do you feel vulnerable to forces beyond your control within a relationship? What insecurities are you harbouring?

POLICE

Authority, justice or fear of punishment; guilt or inferiority

What role did the police play in your dream? Were they threatening or helpful? What might this authority figure be asking you to evaluate in your waking life? Have you behaved unfairly recently or is someone behaving unfairly toward you?

PURSE (OR WALLET)

Empty — fear of loss of a loved one or the security offered by a relationship

Full — richness and comfort in a relationship

What colour was the purse or wallet? What was inside it other than money? If it was empty, what did your dream self expect to find in it? Do you feel in waking life that you have recently lost a friend? Has a relationship been lacking in some way?

RAINBOW

Good news, promise or forgiveness

Were the colours of the rainbow as they appear in waking life? Which emotions could each colour of your dream rainbow represent? What was the scene on the ground beneath the rainbow? Which colour was the sky around the rainbow? Are you experiencing any difficulties in any of your relationships? Have you been unforgiving in some way? If the rainbow represents good news, what news could that be?

STORM

Transition; anger or discord

Were you alone in the dream when the storm broke? If not, who was with you? Were you inside or outside? Did you get drenched? Did the storm feel invigorating or scary? In waking life are you and a friend or your partner going through difficult times or challenging changes? Are you harbouring unexpressed anger against a friend or colleague? How might your dream show you ways to express yourself reasonably?

TEETH

Health; fear of losing a loved one

How were teeth represented in your dream? Were they loose or broken? Or did you find them outside your mouth? In a jar or other receptacle? Are you feeling insecure in a relationship? Are you concerned about your health or happiness?

TRAVEL

Change or exploration

Did your dream emotions feel genial and optimistic or disquieted and unhappy? Were you the one travelling or someone else? What was the mode of transport? Which changes are taking place in your relationships? Are you facing a crucial decision? Are you clearly expressing your views?

WALL

Blocked communication, a desire to maintain individuality or the need for security

What lies on the other side of the wall? Is there a way through the barrier, such as a gap or a gate? Could you climb, jump or fly over it if you tried? Were you happy on your side of the wall or was there a sense of frustration? In waking life how could you communicate more effectively with a friend or partner? Do you feel someone is not listening to you? Do you feel the need to be alone for a while with your thoughts?

WATCH

Slow clock — emotional calmness and quiet

Racing too fast — emotional discord

Who was wearing the watch in your dream? If you are not the watch owner, who did it belong to? Was it old or new, digital or analogue? Was it working properly? What time did it say?

WILD ANIMALS

Passion

Can you identify the animals that appeared? Did they reflect waking life animals or fantasy beasts? How did you feel in their presence — fearful or comfortable? Which aspects of yourself or your desires could they represent? Are you suppressing desire for an individual in your waking life? Are your sexual needs being met by your partner? How did you feel when you woke up — aroused, ashamed or neither?

NOTES